LEARN ANGULAR IN 24 HOURS

A STEP-BY-STEP APPROACH

BY

LAKSHMI KAMALA THOTA

White Falcon Publishing

www.whitefalconpublishing.com

Learn Angular in 24 Hours
Lakshmi Kamala Thota

www.whitefalconpublishing.com

ISBN - 978-93-89932-07-2

Table of Contents

Table of Contents...iii

Preface..vii

Introduction 1

    When to Use Angular...1

    Where to Use Angular 2

    Pre-requisites to Start Angular Development 4

Scenarios and Targets 5

    Scenario 1: Develop a Web Page with Some Content..............5

    Scenario 2: Create a Web Page with Styled Content 6

    Scenario 3: Create a Web Page with a Simple Form 7

    Scenario 4: Create a Logic File with Basic Logic...............7

    Scenario 5: Add Logic to Move Data Between UI & Logic File 8

    Scenario 6: Create Object in Logic, Display Object Details............9

    Scenario 7: Create List in Logic File, Display it on a Web Page 10

    Scenario 8: Display List Info as a Table on a Web Page 10

    Scenario 9: Connect to API, Pull & Display Data 11

    Scenario 10: Understand End to End Flow from DB to UI 12

    Scenario 11: Application with Multiple Pages, Logic Files, Same Logic.........13

    Scenario 12: Application with Web Pages, Same Logic from Service 14

    Scenario 13: Move Angular Application to FTP Server..............14

    Achieving Targets 15

Setting Up the Environment 20

    What to Install to Start Angular development..............20

    Installing Visual Studio Code 21

    Installing Node.JS 25

    Installing Angular CLI 30

Exploring Commands..32

    Commands Used in Angular Development 32

    How to Execute Commands...33

Understanding the Code 36

Angular Project Structure..36
Designing the Application 40
Styling the Application..40
Implementing the Logic 41
Working with Objects 43
Creating an Object 43
Displaying the Object Info 45
Styling the Object Info 47
Working with Lists 49
Creating a List..49
Displaying the List Info 50
Using a For Loop to Loop Through the List 52
Functions and Events...54
Creating Functions 54
Working with Events...55
Calling Functions 55
Working with Forms 58
Passing Values from UI to the Component 58
Passing Values from Component to the UI 60
Configuring the Forms Module 61
Conditions 62
Where to Use Conditions 62
Using If Condition 62
Filtering Data..65
Filtering Scenarios...65
How To Filter Data 66
Classes 70
Creating a Class 70
Creating a Class File 72
Importing the Class 73
Using a Class...73
Interfaces 75
Creating an Interface 75
Importing an Interface 76
Using an Interface..77

Why an Interface and a Class 77
Developing a website 78
Implementing Routing.. 78
Creating Web Pages.. 80
Linking Web Pages 81
Visibility to the world 84
Creating Production Build 84
Working with FTP.. 86
Deploying Files to The Server... 86
Services the Backbone... 89
Why Services 89
Implementing Common Logic.. 90
Calling Service from the Component... 91
Components Deep Dive... 94
Creating Components... 94
Passing Parameters 97
Using Directives 99
Why Directives 99
Using built-In Directives... 100
Creating Custom Directives 102
Working with Pipes.. 105
Why Pipes 105
Built-In Pipes.. 106
Using Built-in Pipes 106
Creating Custom Pipes... 107
Integrating with the API 110
How to Integrate UI with the API 110
Bitcoin Live Mini Project 113
Calling API in the Component 113
Displaying API Results in the Console... 114
Displaying API Results on the UI 116
GitHub Live Users Mini Project.. 118
Calling API in the Component 118
Displaying API Results in the Console... 119
Displaying API Results on the UI 121

Customer Care Mini Project.. 122
    Schematics 122
    Commands and Developing the Application 123
Debugging Code 134
    How to Debug 134
Next Steps 137
    Next Steps to Analyze 137

Preface

There are different types of web development books available in the market today. Only a few books are focused on basics and targeted to absolute beginners who have no idea of coding. The core idea behind this book is to make sure everyone with or without basic knowledge on Angular should understand and expertise web application development using Angular. After going through all chapters, one can quickly and confidently create a live web application using Angular in just a few hours. Simple language is used in this book to make sure everyone who reads this book can understand every concept without any complexity. All concepts in this book are presented with many examples, screenshots through a step-by-step approach. Live mini-project with an assignment at the end of this book, using all the concepts can add extra confidence.

Introduction

Targets for this Hour

- When to Use Angular
- Where to Use Angular
- Prerequisites to Start Angular Development

WHEN TO USE ANGULAR

The most challenging part while planning to develop a web application is decision making on what framework to use for a web application. Obvious choices for selection would be opting for a framework with features like code reusability, mobile/web/native desktop support, performance, community support, etc. One best and suggested choice with all the above features is Angular.

Based on the below analysis from popular search engines, the best recommendation would be to use Angular. Below images are search results from a top online search engine.

> which companies use angular 🎤 🔍

Companies that **use Angular**: **Companies** that **use Angular**: Microsoft, Autodesk, MacDonald's, UPS, Cisco Solution Partner Program, AT&T, Apple, Adobe, GoPro, ProtonMail, Clarity Design System, Upwork, Freelancer, Udemy, YouTube, Paypal, Nike, Google, Telegram, Weather, iStockphoto, AWS, Crunchbase.

Source: Popular search engine

> which framework is most popular 🔍

Which framework is best? ^

Top 5 Frontend Web Development Frameworks to Look At

1. Angular. ...
2. Ember. ...
3. Flutter. ...
4. React. ...
5. Vue.js.

Jun 3, 2019

Source: Popular search engine

WHERE TO USE ANGULAR

Web application development companies generally have a minimum of three common teams. They are the web development team, API development team, database team. Every company has its own set of teams, and the teams mentioned above are standard for most of the companies. The final web application is a combination of efforts by these teams via code and communication. A web developer communicates with other teams to get the required inputs to build the application. The word web developer implies to Angular developer here.

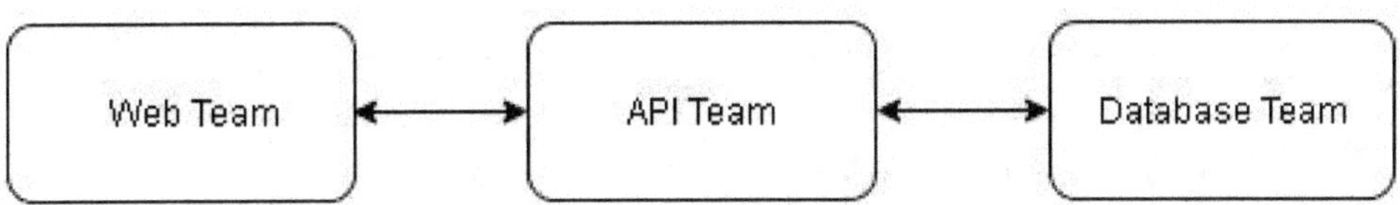

The database team is responsible for working on databases, tables, querying, optimizing data, and other data related operations.

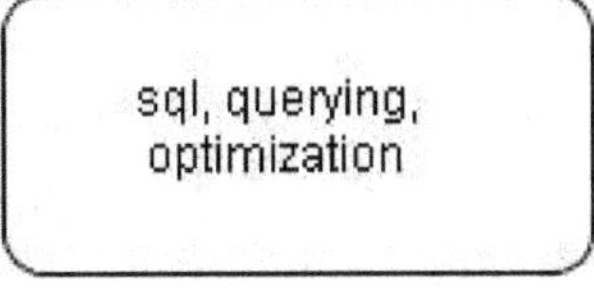

Database Team

API team is responsible for communicating with the database team, and writing code, operations by connecting to the database. This team is also responsible for communicating with the web development team to get requirements and share API links to the web development team. In layman terms, the UI team can expect URLs from the API team. Angular developers should understand how to use the API URLs in their code and display API results on the web pages.

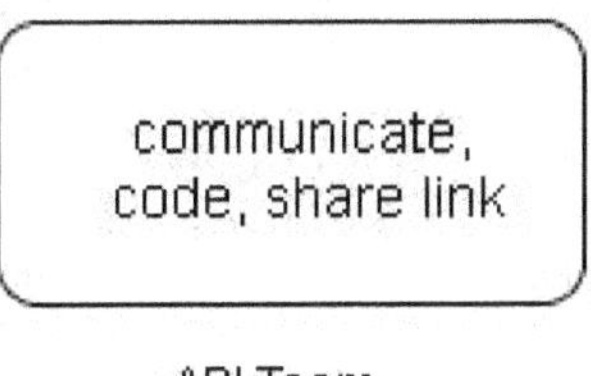

API Team

The web development team is responsible for designing, implementing logic, and data binding. This team is responsible for communicating with the API team to explain the requirements and request related API links. The web team is also responsible for using APIs in the application and displaying relevant information on the web pages.

Web Team

PRE-REQUISITES TO START ANGULAR DEVELOPMENT

Before starting Angular application development, a recommendation is to have some basic understanding of HTML, CSS, Typescript. To Design a web application, developers use HTML. To add styles to the web pages, developers use CSS or LESS. Use JavaScript or typescript to implement the logic for the application.

Scenarios and Targets

Targets for this Hour

- General Web Application Development Scenarios
- Setting Targets to Learn Angular

Basic understanding of general web application development scenarios is required to start learning angular application development. Web development scenarios include one or more cases like searching, filtering, displaying lists, displaying tabular data, paging, sorting etc. Based on generic web development use cases, consider digging through a few scenarios which act as pillars for learning angular development.

SCENARIO 1: DEVELOP A WEB PAGE WITH SOME CONTENT

A web application developed using any technology will have some web pages and content in the pages. A learner needs to understand how to create a web page with content. Use Hypertext Markup language to create a web page using any technology. The same applies to angular application development also. Angular application development requires HTML knowledge to develop web pages.

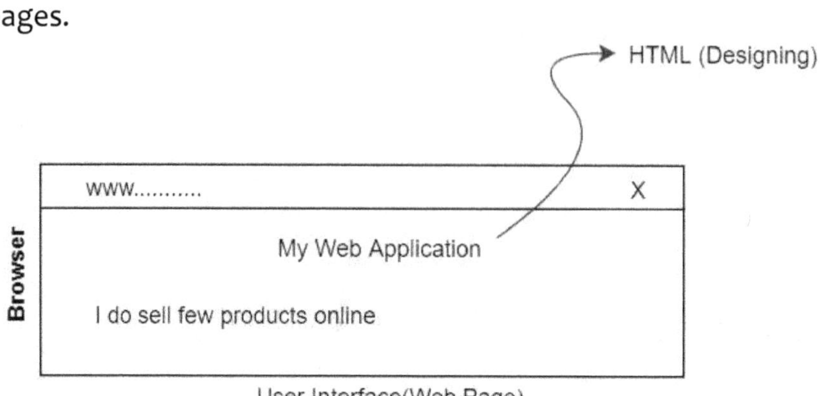

User Interface(Web Page)

To reach the above goal, achieving below targets is mandatory.

Targets
1. Understand how to create a new blank angular application.
2. Understand how to create a web page with sample text using HTML.
3. Understand how to run the angular application and view output in the browser.

SCENARIO 2: CREATE A WEB PAGE WITH STYLED CONTENT

Developing a web page is an essential part of web application development, followed by styling the application. Every web application requires styling to provide end-user with a better look and feel. User experience is the core part of the web page. To add styles to the web page CSS is used. There are many other options like LESS, etc., to add styles to the web application.

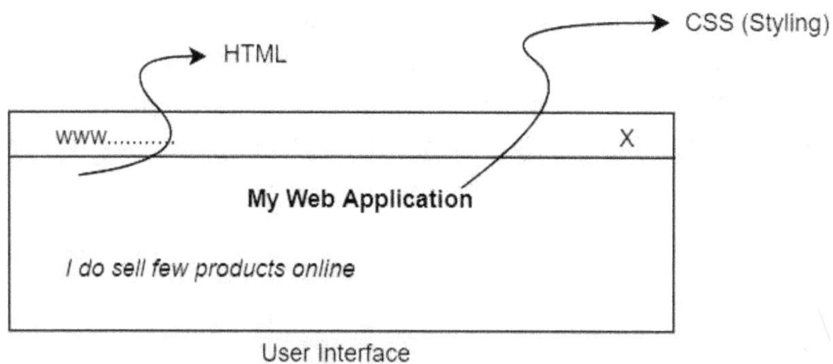

User Interface

To reach the above goal, achieving below targets is mandatory.

Targets
1. Understand how to create a new angular application with an HTML page
2. Understand how to style the HTML elements using CSS

SCENARIO 3: CREATE A WEB PAGE WITH A SIMPLE FORM

Many web applications deal with data passing scenarios from one file to another file. 'Forms' concept act as a place holder for data passing between files. Few general scenarios with forms usage include but not limited to 'Log in', 'Register', 'Compose Email', 'Contact Us Form' etc., Angular developers use forms and data passing scenarios in many cases during application development.

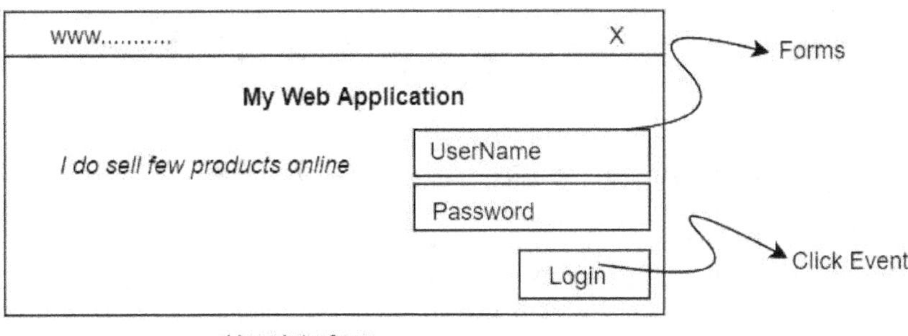

User Interface

To reach the above goal, achieving below targets is mandatory.

Targets
1. Understand how to create an Angular application with a login form using HTML, CSS
2. Understand how to add a 'Click' event to the 'Login' button.

SCENARIO 4: CREATE A LOGIC FILE WITH BASIC LOGIC

Implementing logic is like the heart of Angular application development. Angular developer spends most of the time writing logic using TypeScript. It is recommended to write code once and reuse it multiple times and in various places in the file. Functions solve the purpose of grouping code to a single unit and invoke it when required. The logic file can have multiple functions. Each function will have typescript logic inside it. Events are required to call a function. Few events include but not limited to 'button click', 'mouseover' etc., An action like button click from the HTML code will invoke function written in the logic file.

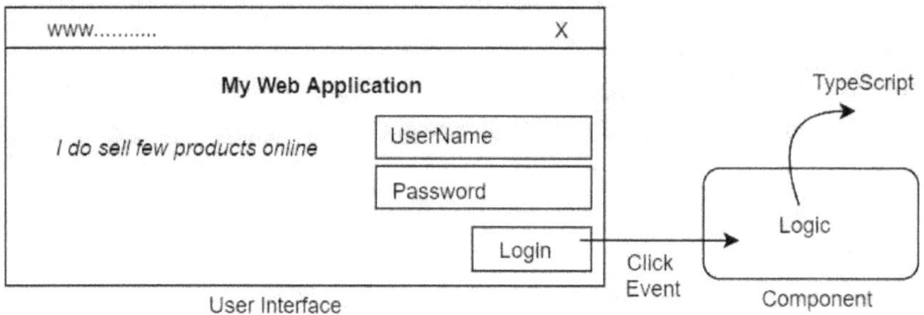

To reach the above goal, achieving below targets is mandatory.

Targets
1. Understand how to create a logic file.
2. Understand how to add simple logic to the logic file.
3. Understand how to make the simple code block as a reusable function.
4. Understand how to invoke the function in the logic file on clicking the login button in the design file.

SCENARIO 5: ADD LOGIC TO MOVE DATA BETWEEN UI & LOGIC FILE

Developers should have a basic idea on how to read user input values in the logic file from a web page and vice versa. Building logic by Implementing calculations, conditions, etc., in the logic file, plays a core role during application development.

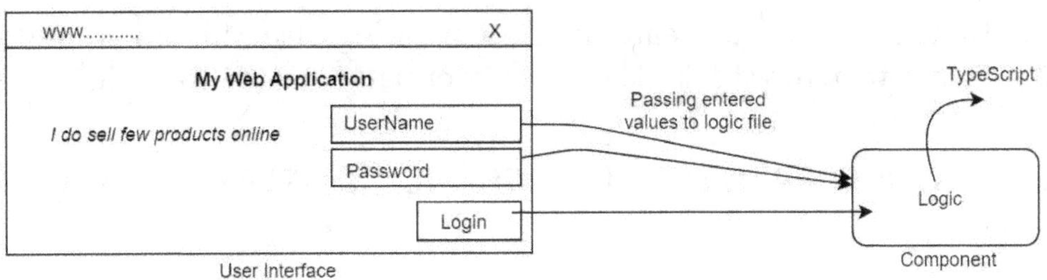

To reach the above goal, achieving below targets is mandatory.

Targets
1. Understand how to pass values from web page to the Logic file.
2. Understand how to pass values from Logic file to web page.
3. Understand how to write the logic in the logic file with the values we get from the textboxes.

SCENARIO 6: CREATE OBJECT IN LOGIC, DISPLAY OBJECT DETAILS

All angular applications will involve using objects in many scenarios. Understanding objects and using them in the logic, webpages is must for an Angular developer.

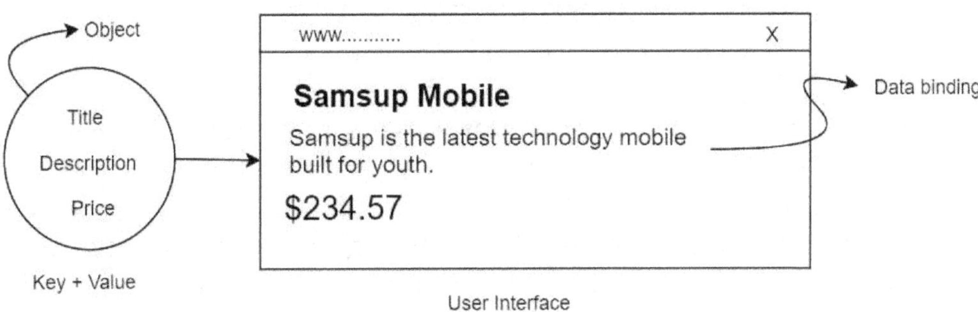

To reach the above goal, achieving below targets is mandatory.

Targets

1. Understand how to create an object in the logic file with few properties.
2. Understand how to display Object information on the web page.

SCENARIO 7: CREATE LIST IN LOGIC FILE, DISPLAY IT ON A WEB PAGE

Using lists in a web application is a very common scenario. Understanding of indexes and loops are mandatory to work with lists. Filters are used on top of the list to display only required items on the web page.

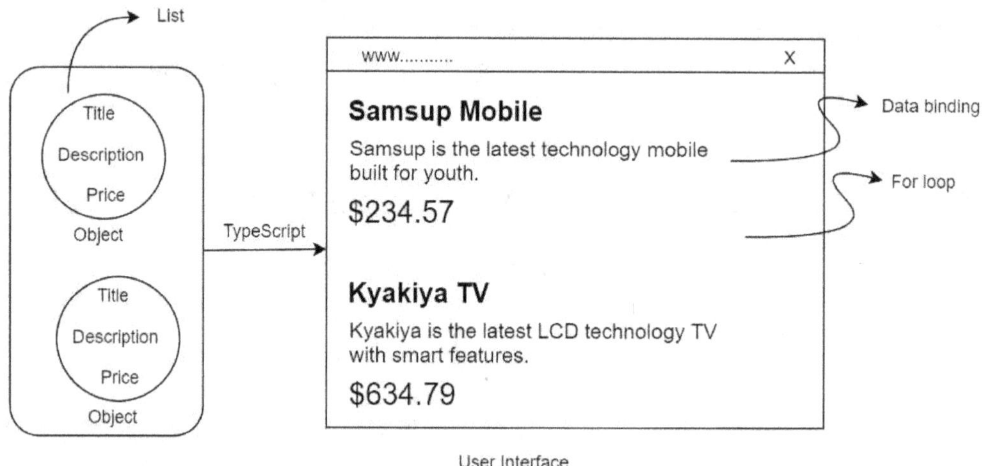

User Interface

To reach the above goal, achieving below targets is mandatory.

Targets

1. Understand how to create a List in the logic file with few properties.
2. Understand how to display List information on the web page.

SCENARIO 8: DISPLAY LIST INFO AS A TABLE ON A WEB PAGE

Displaying a list of items on the web page can in many formats. Based on the requirements list items can be displayed one below another or in the tabular

10

format. Library called 'material' syncs well with Angular applications to generate code to display tables with pre-defined code for paging, sorting, etc.,

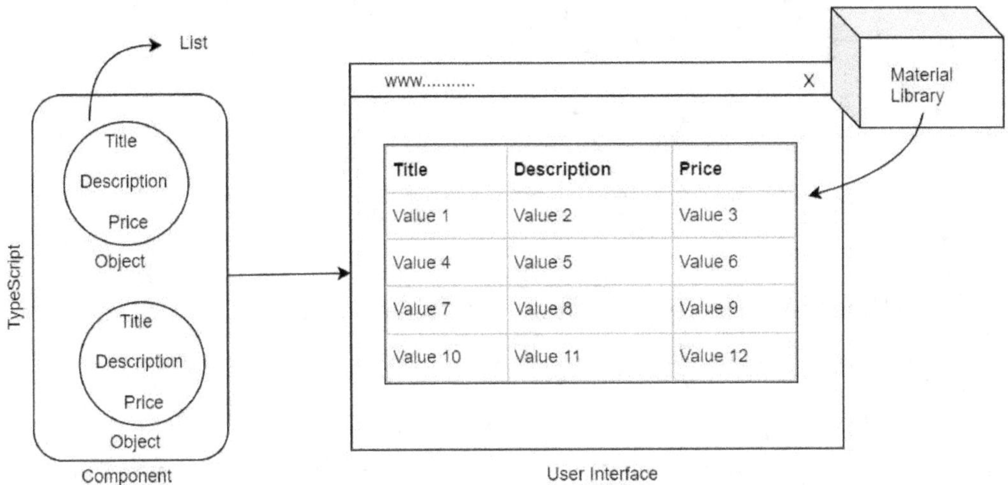

To reach the above goal, achieving below targets is mandatory.

Targets
1. Understand how to install Material library in Angular application.
2. Understand how to create a List in the logic file.
3. Understand how to display list information in the table format on the web page.
4. Understand how to implement paging, sorting to the tabular data on the web page.

SCENARIO 9: CONNECT TO API, PULL & DISPLAY DATA

In a very few situations, the code developed will be used only by the same team, but in many scenarios, the code will be used by external teams as well. APIs will solve the purpose of exposing common functionality across the different teams. Angular developers often talk to the API through code to get the response from it, use the response in the logic file and finally display it on the web page.

11

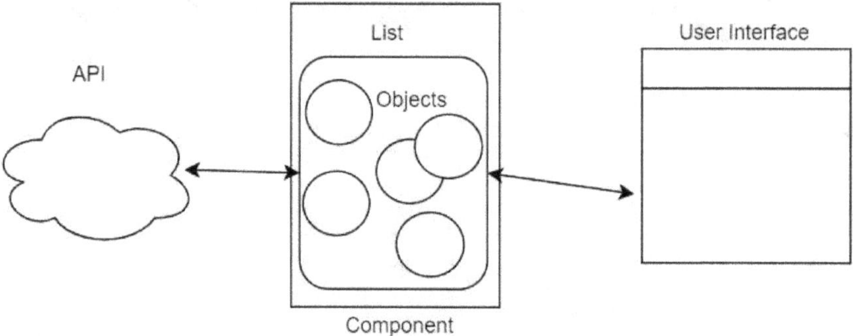

To reach the above goal, achieving below targets is mandatory.

Targets
1. Understand how to call API in the logic file
2. Understand what type of result or response we get from API call
3. Understand how to bind the API response data to the UI

SCENARIO 10: UNDERSTAND END TO END FLOW FROM DB TO UI

The scope of this book is only to understand developing angular applications. An Angular developer needs to understand the end to end flow even if they are not working on DB or API. General web application development scenarios are based on to and fro data passing between database to user interface and vice versa.

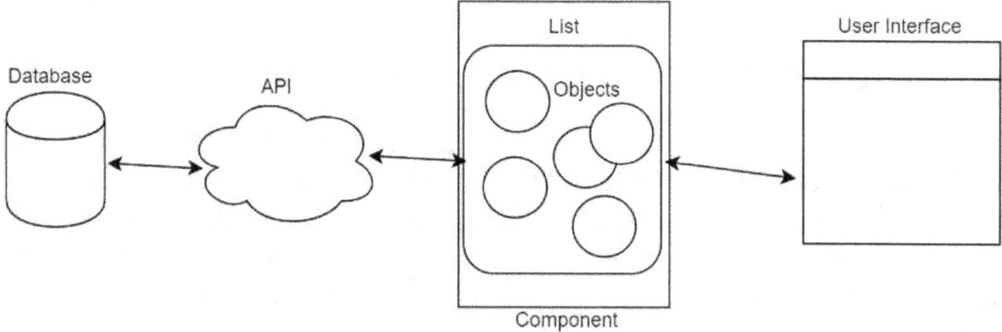

To reach the above goal, achieving below targets is mandatory.

Targets
1. Understanding the end to end process from the database to the user interface. Our scope in this book is not related to the database.

SCENARIO 11: APPLICATION WITH MULTIPLE PAGES, LOGIC FILES, SAME LOGIC

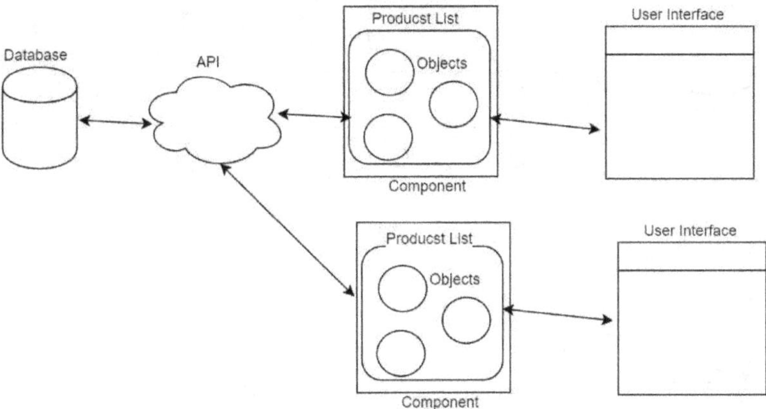

Angular experts recommend starting Angular with a single web page and a single logic file. Learning how to create multiple web pages with logic will be the next step. Typical applications consist of multiple web pages, and each page will have respective logic involved. Developers should have a strong idea of creating and working with multiple webpages and logic files.

To reach the above goal, achieving below targets is mandatory.

Targets
1. Understand how to create multiple components
2. Understand how to write the same logic in various components

SCENARIO 12: APPLICATION WITH WEB PAGES, SAME LOGIC FROM SERVICE

Consider an application having multiple webpages and few pages having the same logic. It is recommended not to write the same code in multiple web pages or logic files. Instead, create a 'service' to add common code and call service in required logic files.

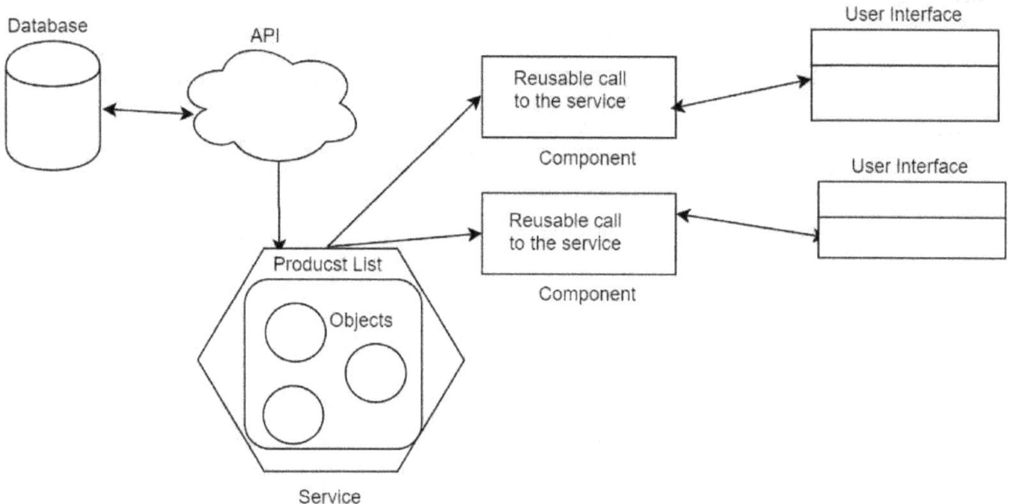

To reach the above goal, achieving below targets is mandatory.

Targets
1. Understand how to create a service and create reusable code instead of writing in multiple places in the component.

SCENARIO 13: MOVE ANGULAR APPLICATION TO FTP SERVER

The angular application developers created should be published to the web to make it available online. Deployment can be a manual or automated process. Developers should be familiar with the list of all files that are part of the deployment and how to deploy required files.

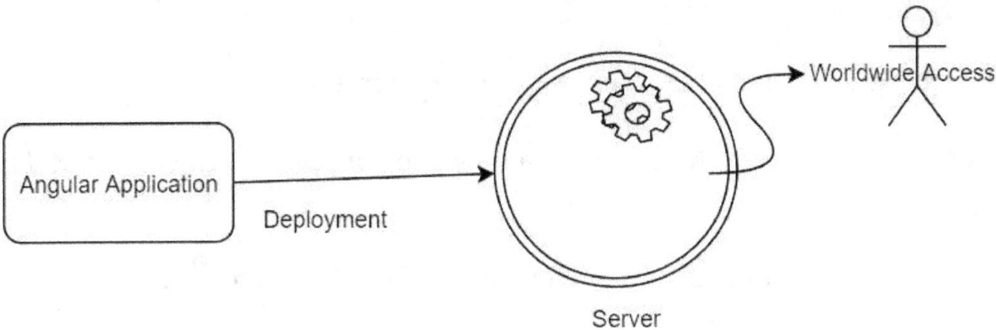

To reach the above goal, achieving below targets is mandatory.

Targets
1. Understand how to move your angular application from local computer to live server so that everyone in the world can view it.

ACHIEVING TARGETS

Setting up targets is the first step in the learning roadmap. An Angular developer's ultimate goal is to achieve the planned targets. Next chapters cover all the targets with screenshots and examples. Below are the list of targets and respective covered chapters for reference.

Target 1 Understand how to create a new blank angular application.

'How to execute commands', 'Understanding the code' chapters covers this target.

Target 2 Understand how to create a web page with sample text using HTML.

'Understanding the code' chapter covers this target. This target is not part of the angular application development.

Target 3 Understand how to run the application and view output in the browser.

'How to execute commands' chapter covers this target.

Target 4 Understand how to create a new angular application with an HTML page.

'How to execute commands', 'Understanding the code' chapters cover these targets.

Target 5 Understand how to style the HTML elements using CSS.

'Understanding the code' chapter covers this target.

Target 6 Understand how to create an Angular application with a login form using HTML, CSS.

'Working with forms' chapter covers this target.

Target 7 Understand how to add a 'click' event to the 'Login' button.

'Functions and events' chapter covers this target.

Target 8 Understand how to create a logic file.

'Understanding the code' chapter covers this target.

Target 9 Understand how to add simple logic to the logic file.

'Understanding the code' chapter covers this target.

Target 10 Understand how to make the simple log code block a reusable function.

'Functions and events', 'Components deep dive', chapters cover this target.

Target 11 Understand how to invoke the function in the logic file on clicking the login button.

'Functions and events' chapter covers this target.

Target 12 Understand how to pass values from the web page to the Logic file.

'How to execute commands', 'Understanding the code' chapters cover this target.

Target 13 Understand how to pass values from Logic file to web page.

'Working with forms' chapter covers this target.

Target 14 Understand how to write the logic in logic file with the values we get from the textboxes.

'Working with forms' chapter covers this target.

Target 15 Understand how to create an object in the logic file with few properties.

'Classes', 'Interfaces' chapters cover this target.

Target 16 Understand how to display Object information on the web page.

'Working with Objects' covers this topic.

Target 17 Understand how to create a List in the logic file with few properties.

'Working with Lists' cover this target.

Target 18 Understand how to display List information on the web page.

'Working with Lists' chapter cover this target.

Target 19 Understand how to install Material library in Angular application.

'Customer Care mini-project' chapter covers this target.

Target 20 Understand how to create a List in the logic file.

'Working with Lists' chapter cover this target.

Target 21 Understand how to display list information in the table format on the web page.

'Customer Care mini-project' chapter covers this target.

Target 22 Understand how to implement paging, sorting to the tabular data on the web page.

'Customer Care mini-project' chapter covers this target.

Target 23 Understand how to call API in the logic file.

'Integrating with the API' chapter covers this target.

Target 24 Understand the type of result or response we get from API call.

'Integrating with the API' chapter covers this target.

Target 25 Understand how to bind the API response data to the UI.

'Integrating with the API' chapter covers this target.

Target 26 Understanding the end to end process from the database to the user interface. Our scope in this book is not related to the database.

Understanding End to end is part of one or more chapters except for the database connectivity.

Target 27 Understand how to Create multiple components.

'Components deep dive' chapter covers this target.

Target 28 Understand how to write the same logic in multiple components.

'Services the backbone' chapter covers this target.

Target 29 Understand how to create a service and create reusable code instead of writing in multiple places in the component.

'Services the backbone' chapter covers this target.

Target 30 Understand how to move your angular application from local computer to live server so that everyone in the world can view it.

'Visibility to the world' covers this target.

Setting Up the Environment

Targets for this Hour

- What to Install
- Installing Visual Studio Code
- Installing NodeJS
- Installing Angular CLI

WHAT TO INSTALL TO START ANGULAR DEVELOPMENT

To work on Angular application development, the developer needs an integrated development environment. There are many IDEs available online, but not all of them are lightweight and easy to use.

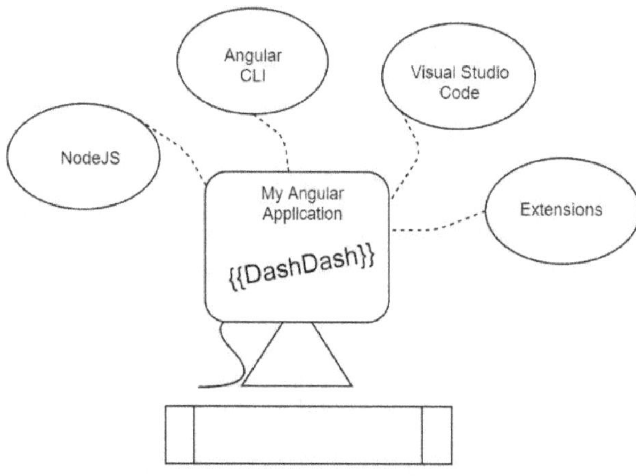

One best and preferred IDE for Angular application development is 'Visual Studio Code'. Angular experts recommend using the Visual Studio Code to develop Angular applications.

INSTALLING VISUAL STUDIO CODE

Visual studio code is free and lightweight IDE with tons for options available to develop Angular web applications. Downloading and Installing visual studio code is free and straightforward. To start Angular application development, follow the below steps to install visual studio code IDE.

Step 1: Search for "download visual **studio code**" in any search engine online.

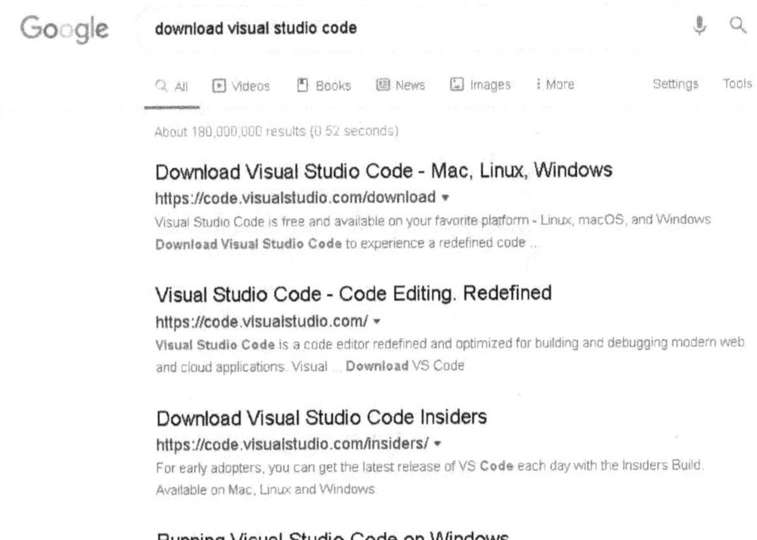

Step 2: Select a related and trusted download link. It should redirect to the Microsoft website with download options.

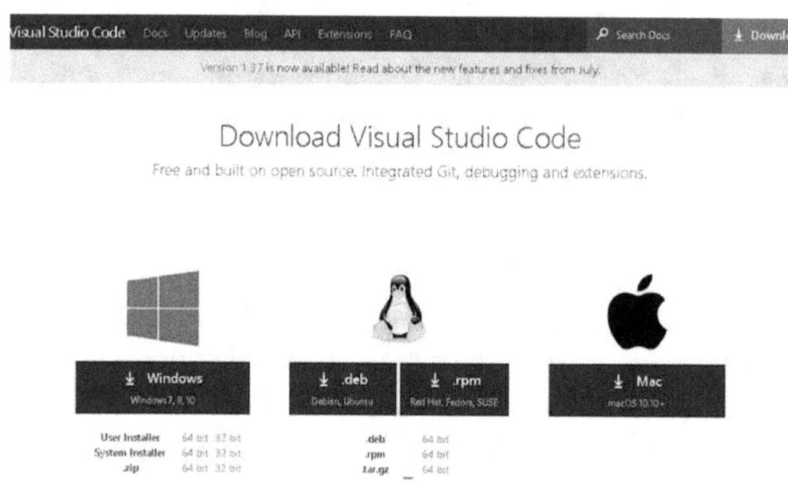

Step 3: Based on the current operating system and bit, click on the related link.

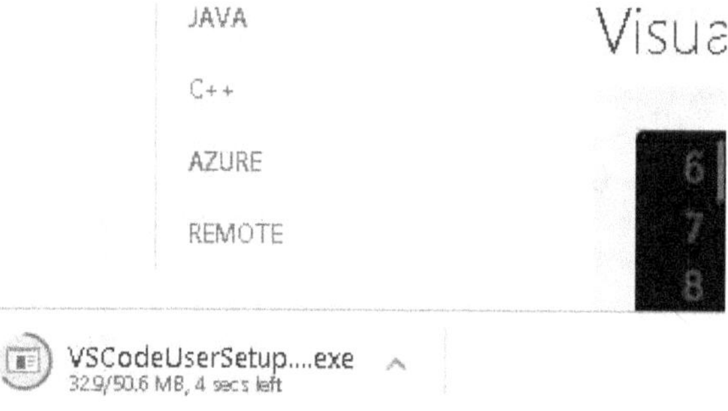

Step 4: Once the 'exe' file downloading process completes, open the file by clicking on the down arrow next to the downloaded file name.

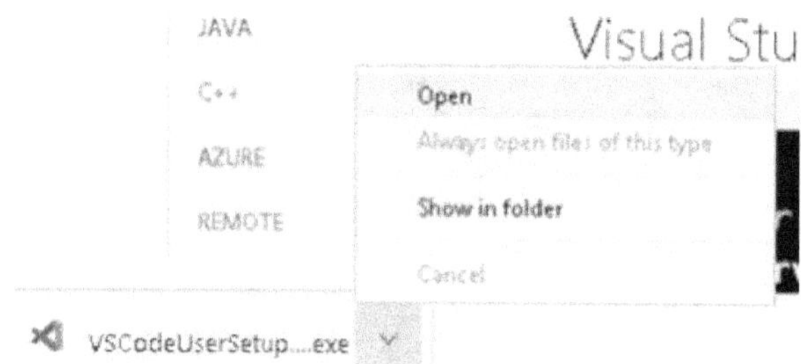

Step 5: Read the license agreement, select 'I accept' if agreement looks good, and click the 'Next' button.

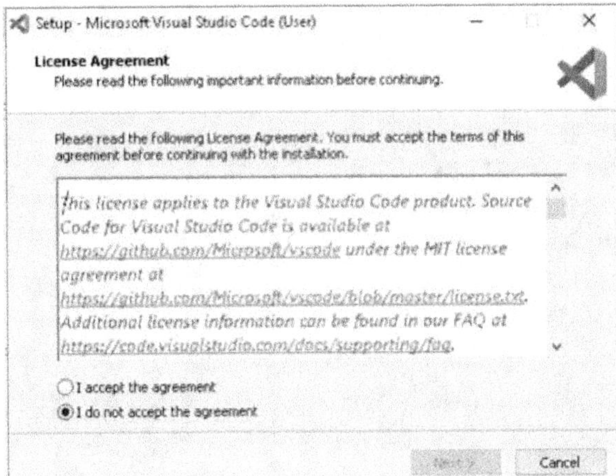

Step 6: Select the required additional tasks and click Next

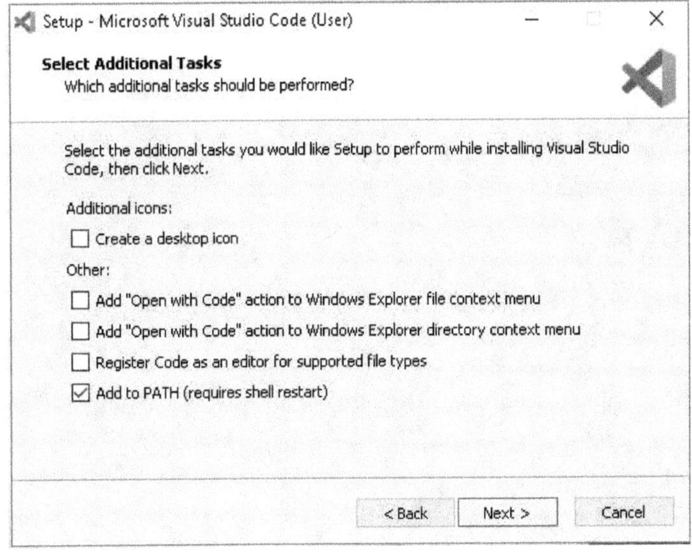

Step 7: Click install

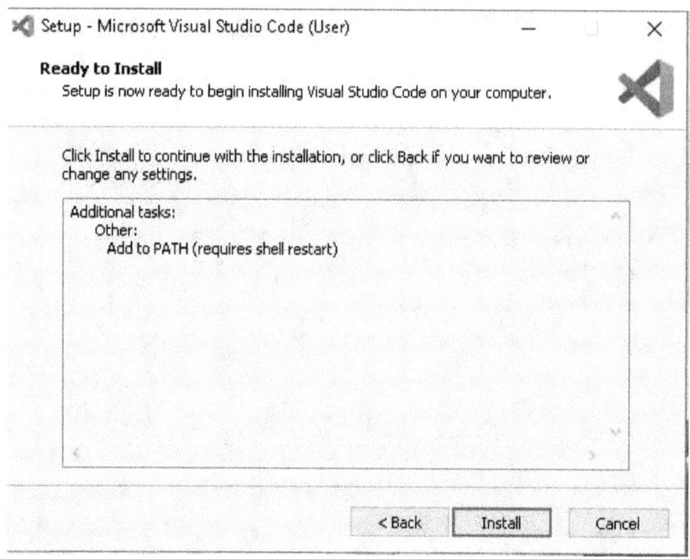

Step 8: Relax visual studio code installation is in progress.

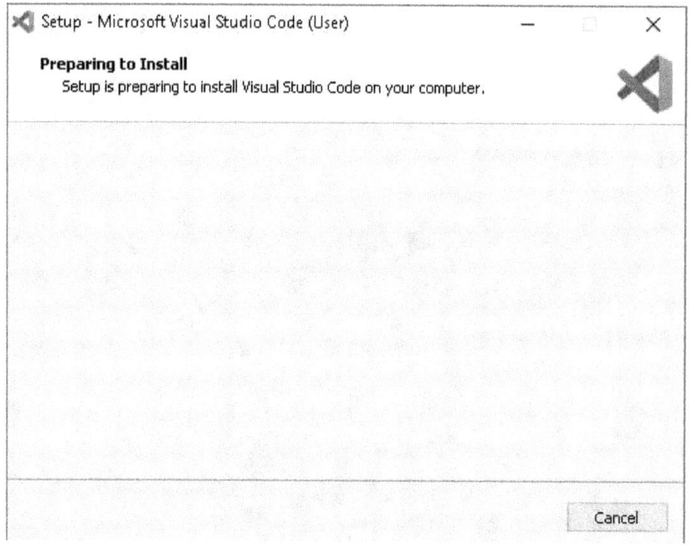

Step 9: Keep an eye on the progress.

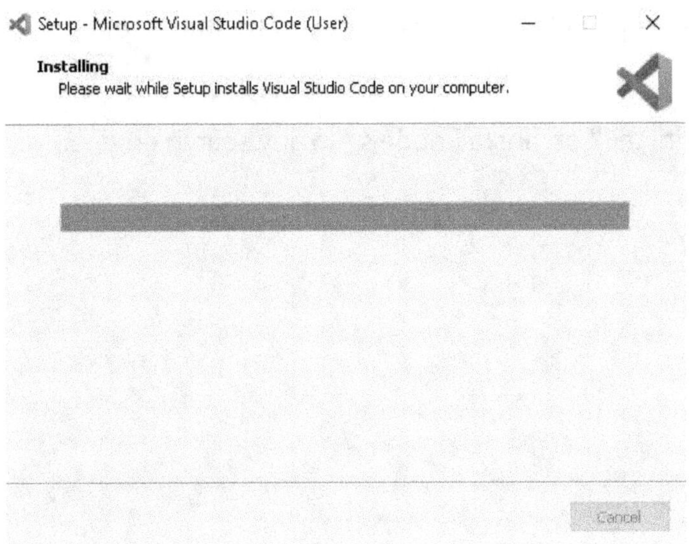

Step 10: Once done, click the 'Finish' button to load the Visual studio code.

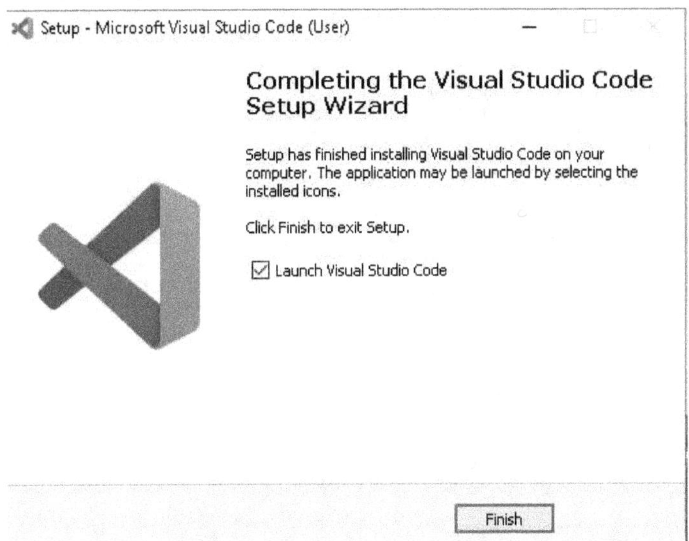

INSTALLING NODE.JS

To work on Angular development, developers should install Node.JS (NodeJS). NodeJS is a JavaScript runtime built on chrome's v8 JavaScript engine. Node.JS is open-source. Follow the steps below to install NodeJS to start the Angular application development.

Step 1: Search for "nodejs install" or "install nodejs" in any search engine.

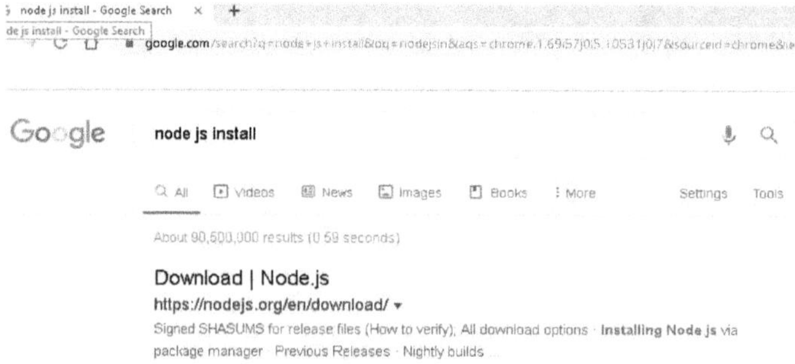

Step 2: Based on the current operating system and bit, select a related download link.

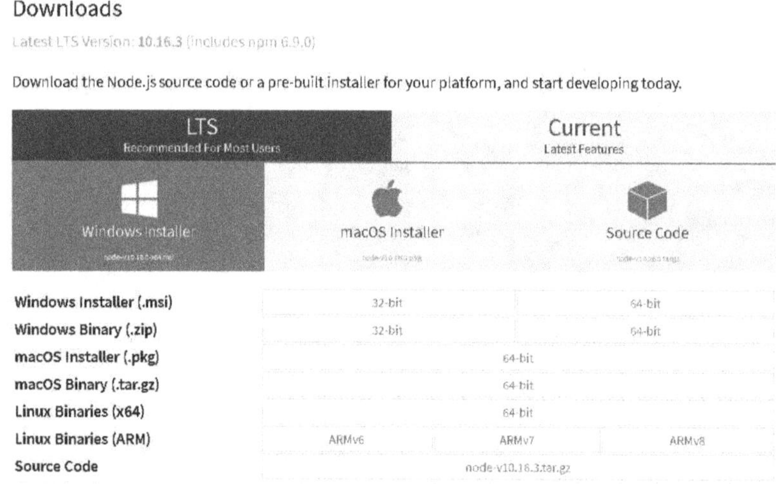

Step3: Wait till the installation file downloads.

macOS Installer (.pkg)
macOS Binary (.tar.gz)
Linux Binaries (x64)
Linux Binaries (ARM)

node-v10.16.3-x64.msi
17.3/17.3 MB

Step 4: Once the downloading process completes, open the downloaded file.

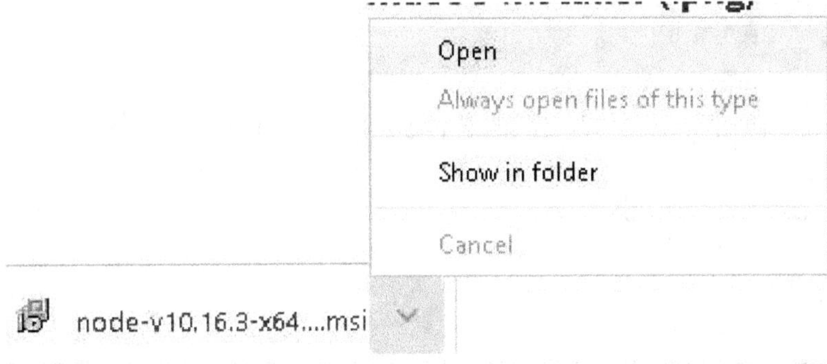

Step 5: Please wait until the "Next" button is active.

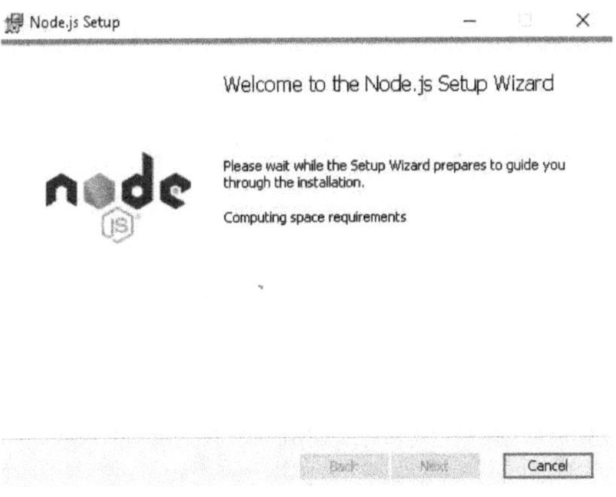

Step 6: Click the 'Next' button.

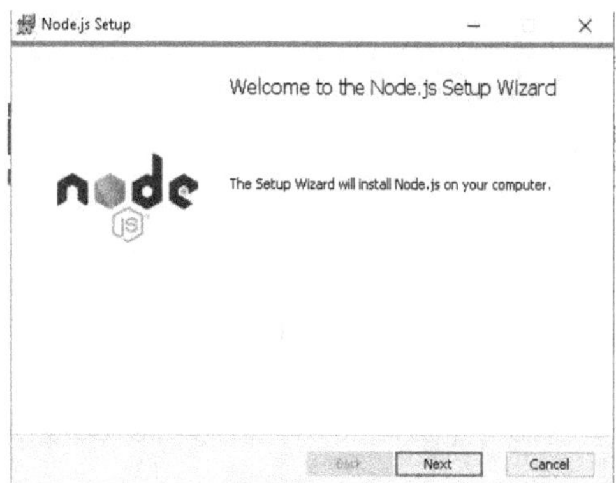

Step 7: Read the license and select 'I Accept' if the agreement looks good.

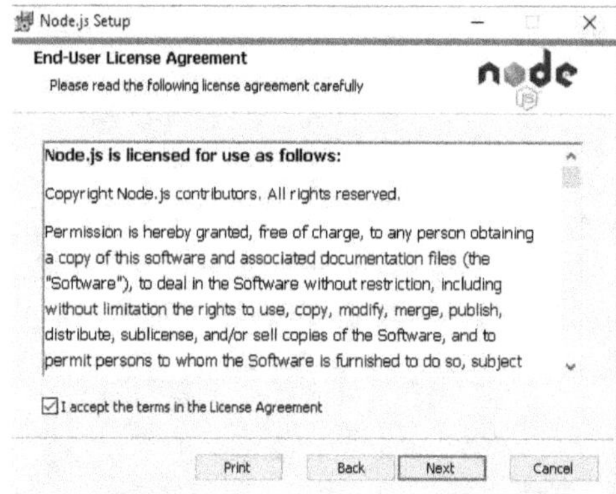

Step 8: Use the default path to install NodeJs or change the path if required.

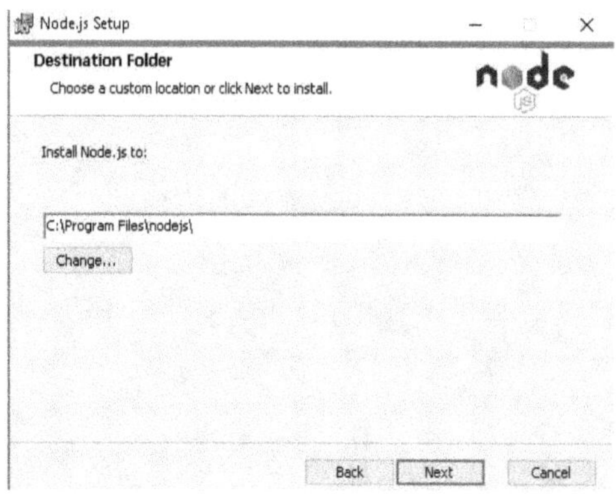

Step 9: Click the 'Next' button with selected options.

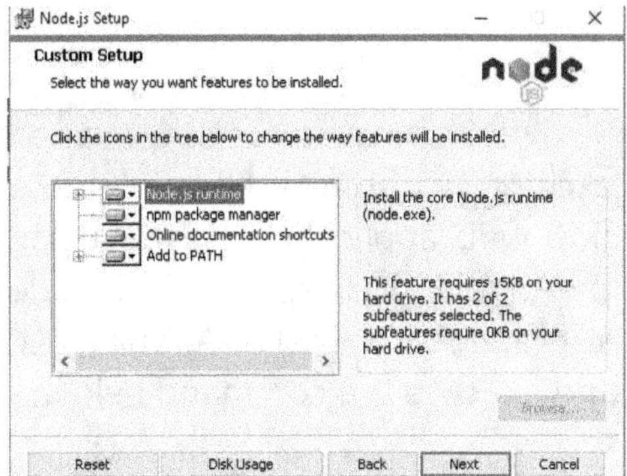

Step 10: Click Install, wait until the installation completes.

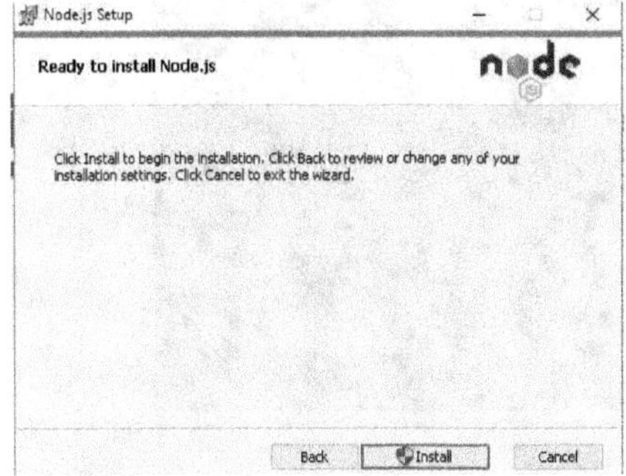

Step 11: Click Finish to complete NodeJS installation on the machine. Restart the computer.

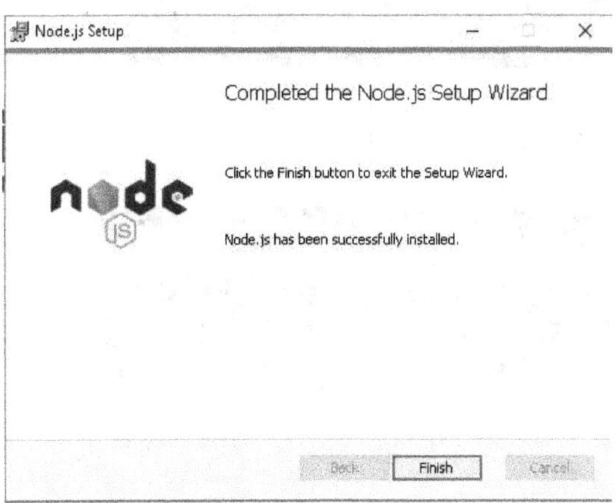

INSTALLING ANGULAR CLI

Creating quick web applications is always exciting. A command-line interface for Angular helps web developers to develop web applications faster using specific commands. The best feature with Angular CLI is, the final code generated with commands comes with best practices. To install Angular CLI, open the terminal in the visual studio code and execute the command below.

Step 1: Open Visual Studio Code and select 'New Terminal.'

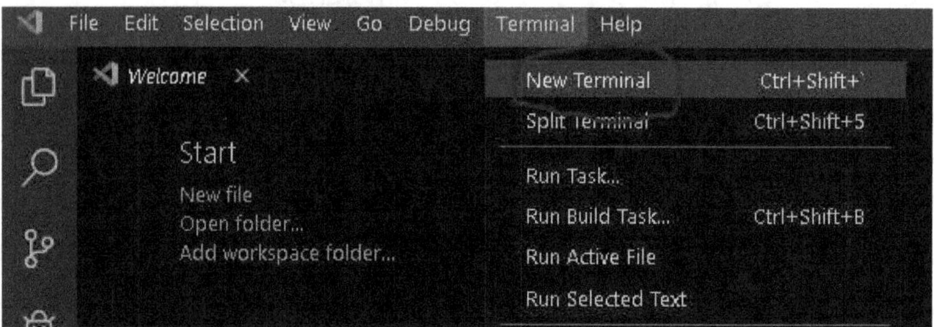

Step 2: The terminal window positions at the bottom part of the visual studio code.

Step 3: Type the below command to install Angular CLI.

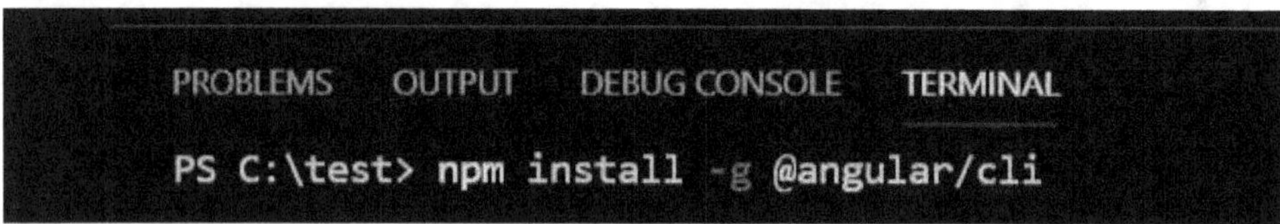

Step 4: Press the 'enter' button.

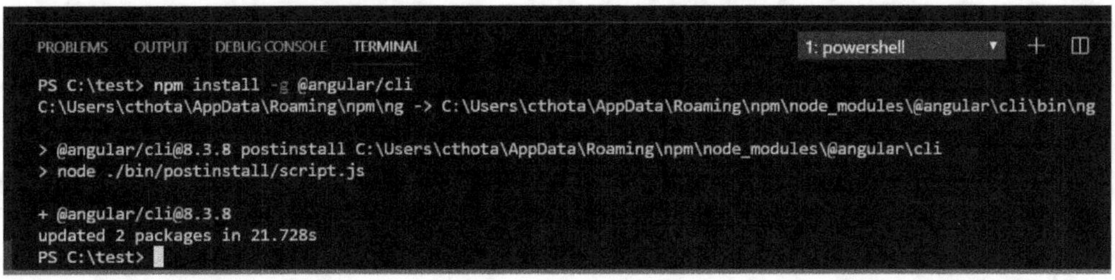

The above steps conclude the basic environment setup required for Angular application development.

Exploring Commands

Targets for this Hour

- Commands to Use
- How to Execute Commands

COMMANDS USED IN ANGULAR DEVELOPMENT

Operations like creating, developing, building, generating an Angular application depend on commands. Execute these commands in the terminal in visual studio code. Developers should have a good grip on these commands to make the application development process smooth and straightforward.

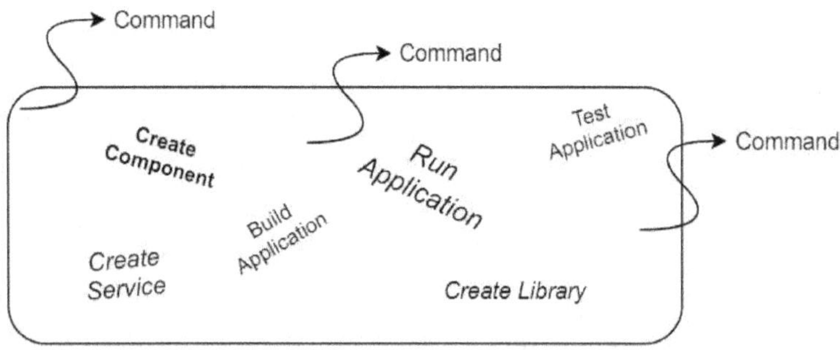

It is difficult to explain all commands in this book, but below are the few most used commands during essential phases of Angular application development.

- ng new <application Name> ⇨ To create a new application
- ng generate component <component name> ⇨ To create new component
- ng generate service <service name> ⇨To create a service
- ng serve --open ⇨ Build and open the application in the web browser
- ng build --prod ⇨ To compress and generate prod version files
- ng add @Angular/material ⇨ To install Angular material
- ng generate @Angular/material:<item type> <item name> ⇨ To add Angular material object/items
- ctrl + c ⇨ terminate the command or the execution
- ng help ⇨ to view all commands information

HOW TO EXECUTE COMMANDS

The initial step is to focus on a few commands and results when the commands execute in visual studio code. To execute any of the above commands, select the 'New **terminal**' option from the 'Terminal' menu in visual studio code. Once the terminal opens, type the required command and press enter. Press enter to execute the command.

The next step is to focus on operations like creating a new application, building the application, running the application using some of the above commands. Open terminal, enter the command to create a new application, press enter.

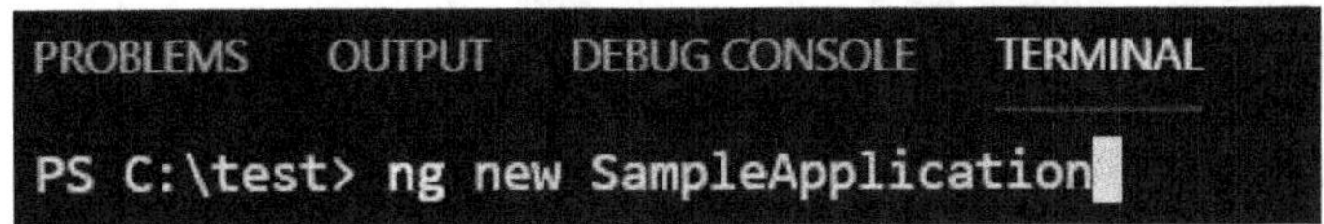

Enter 'Y', and press enter key twice.

```
PROBLEMS    OUTPUT    DEBUG CONSOLE    TERMINAL

PS C:\test> ng new SampleApplication
? Would you like to add Angular routing? No
? Which stylesheet format would you like to use? (Use arrow keys)
> CSS
  SCSS   [ https://sass-lang.com/documentation/syntax#scss                ]
  Sass   [ https://sass-lang.com/documentation/syntax#the-indented-syntax ]
  Less   [ http://lesscss.org                                             ]
  Stylus [ http://stylus-lang.com                                         ]
```

Wait till the application creation process completes.

```
PROBLEMS    OUTPUT    DEBUG CONSOLE    TERMINAL                          1: node    ▼

CREATE SampleApplication/src/app/app.component.spec.ts (1014 bytes)
CREATE SampleApplication/src/app/app.component.ts (221 bytes)
CREATE SampleApplication/src/app/app.component.css (0 bytes)
CREATE SampleApplication/e2e/protractor.conf.js (810 bytes)
CREATE SampleApplication/e2e/tsconfig.json (214 bytes)
CREATE SampleApplication/e2e/src/app.e2e-spec.ts (650 bytes)
CREATE SampleApplication/e2e/src/app.po.ts (262 bytes)
[    .................] - fetchMetadata: sill pacote range manifest for is-glob@^4.0.0 fetched in 199ms
```

Once the application creation process completes, use the "cls" command to clear the terminal screen. This command is optional.

```
PROBLEMS    OUTPUT    DEBUG CONSOLE    TERMINAL


The file will have its original line endings in your working directory
warning: LF will be replaced by CRLF in tsconfig.json.
The file will have its original line endings in your working directory
warning: LF will be replaced by CRLF in tsconfig.spec.json.
The file will have its original line endings in your working directory
warning: LF will be replaced by CRLF in tslint.json.
The file will have its original line endings in your working directory
    Successfully initialized git.
PS C:\test> cls
```

Use the command 'ng build' to build the application

```
PROBLEMS    OUTPUT    DEBUG CONSOLE    TERMINAL


PS C:\test> ng build
```

Always navigate to the project folder to run any command in the project. Based on the error below, change directory and run commands inside the project directory.

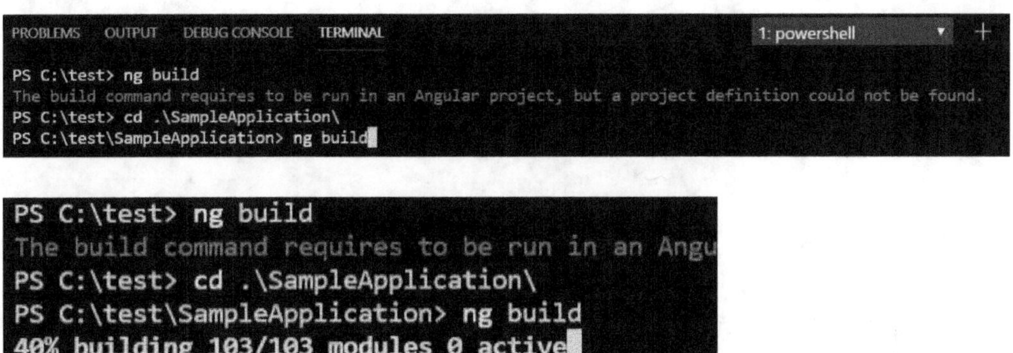

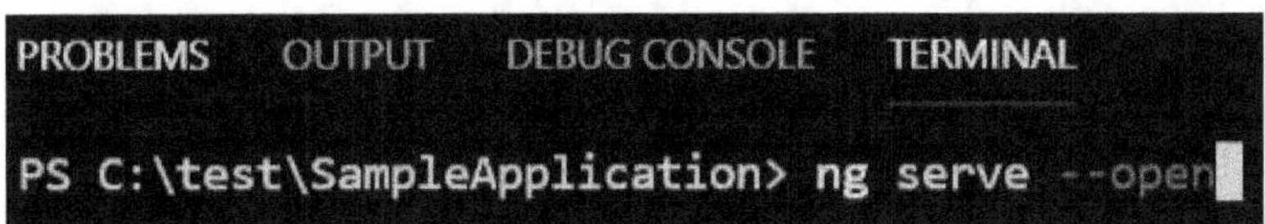

Use the command 'ng serve –open' to build and run the application.

A default web page provided by the Angular CLI template displays the output on the browser.

Understanding the Code

Targets for this Hour

- Angular Project Structure
- Designing the Application
- Styling the Application
- Implementing the Logic

ANGULAR PROJECT STRUCTURE

It is time to understand a little deeper than explored as part of the previous chapter.

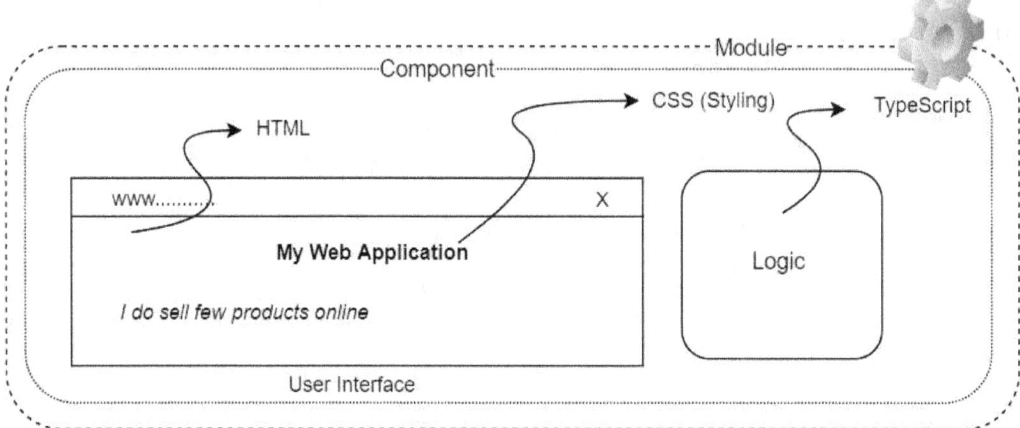

The first step before starting Angular development is to create a new project. To create a new project in Angular, follow the steps below.

Step 1: Create a folder on the desktop or any folder where the application resides.

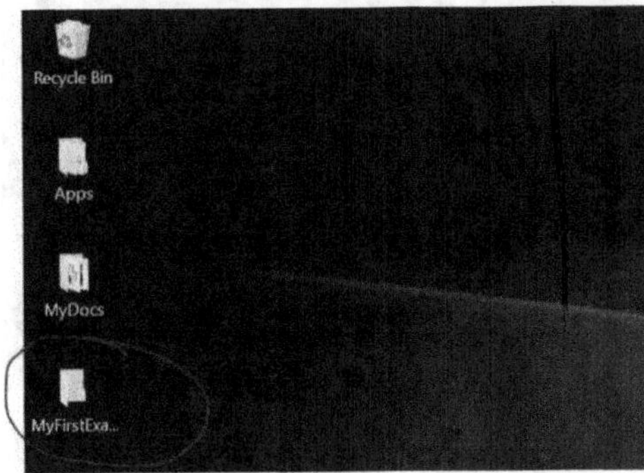

Step 2: Click on the 'Terminal' menu and select 'New Terminal'.

Step 3: Open Folder and points the commands to the created new folder. To do this, select the 'File' menu, **select 'Open Folder',** and select folder from desktop or any folder based on the above point 1.

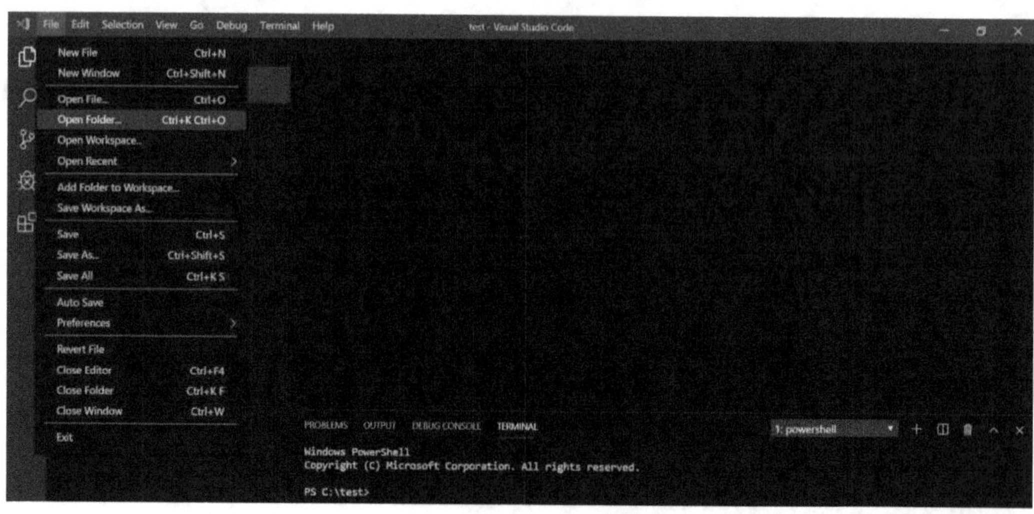

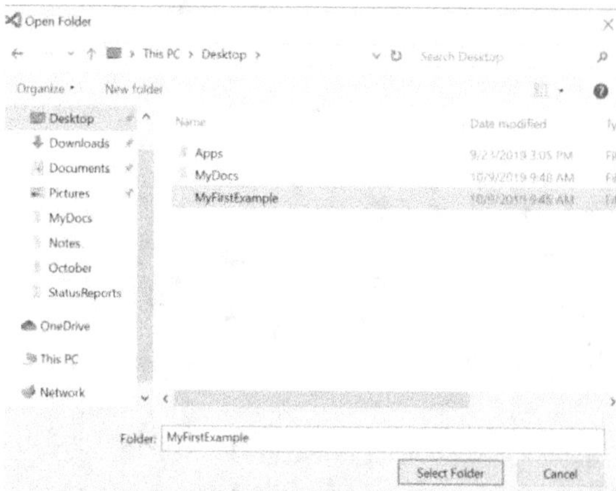

Step 4: Use command "ng new **ProjectName**" to create a new project

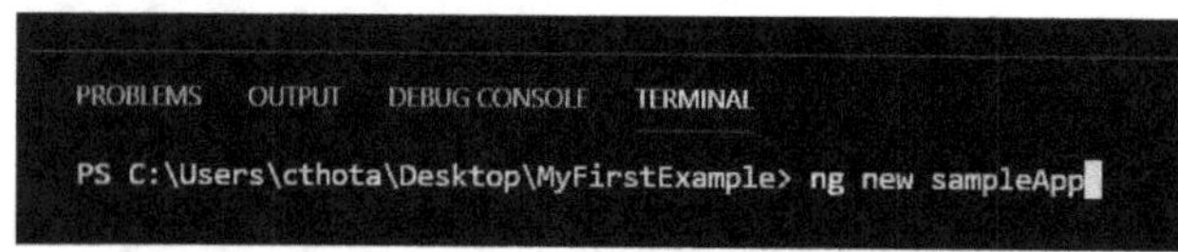

Follow steps, as mentioned in the previous chapter.

Step 5: Created **project's folder** structure looks like the below

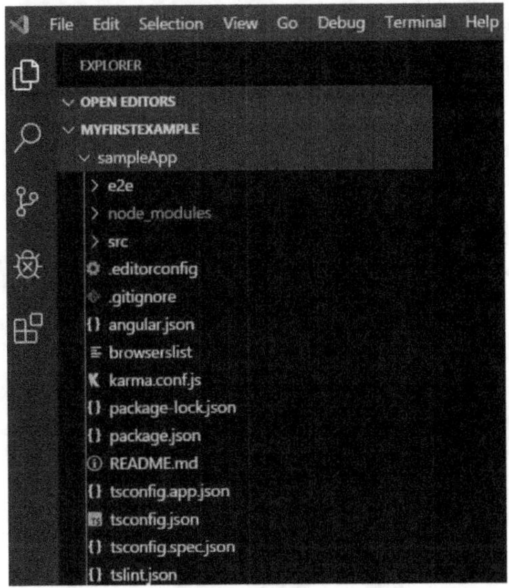

Files mostly used to write code are inside the folder src/app. Based on the folders created, code is written mainly in 3 files, HTML, CSS, TS files. Other files generated are also essential but not as crucial as the mentioned three files. Designing, styling, implementing logic are three main phases of the application development.

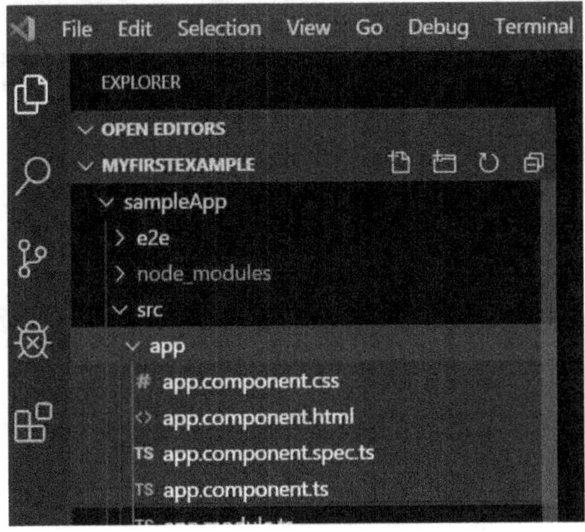

src

    ⇨ app

        ⇨ app.component.css (To add styles)

        ⇨ app.component.html (To add page design)

        ⇨ app.component.spec.ts (To add test cases)

        ⇨ app.component.ts (To add business logic)

Adding test cases is a secondary part of the application development. The scope of this book is limited to web application development and not writing test cases for the Angular application.

DESIGNING THE APPLICATION

Part of the web pages a user can view with eyes in a web application is the user interface. UI includes the design phase of the web application development. The 'ng new' command creates a root HTML file 'app.component.html' by default. Use HTML tags to design the required web page. To expertise in this phase, developers should use HTML skills. In the example below, use HTML tag '<H1>' to display bold text. Add this HTML code in the app.component.html file.

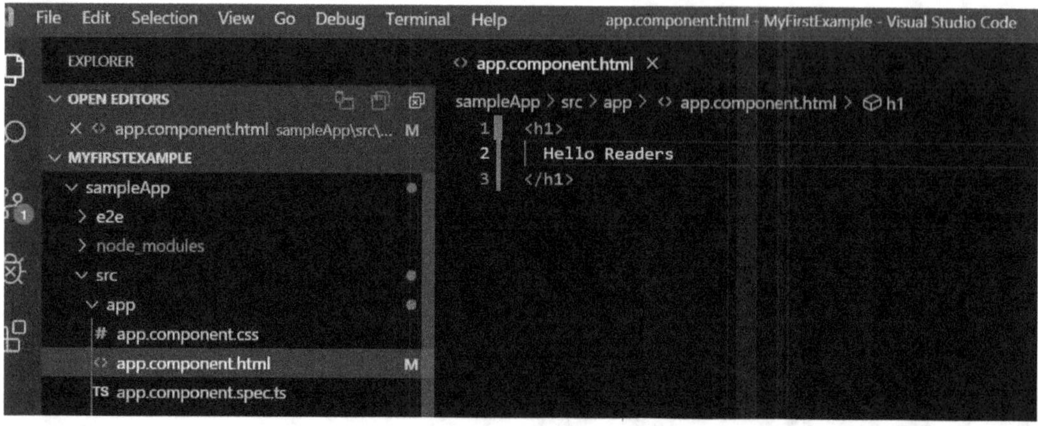

STYLING THE APPLICATION

Adding styles to the web application is part of the styling phase of web application development. The default 'ng new' command creates a root CSS file 'app.component.css'. Use CSS to style the required web pages. Angular developers should be good at adding classes, and ids to HTML elements, understanding CSS classes to expertise in this phase.

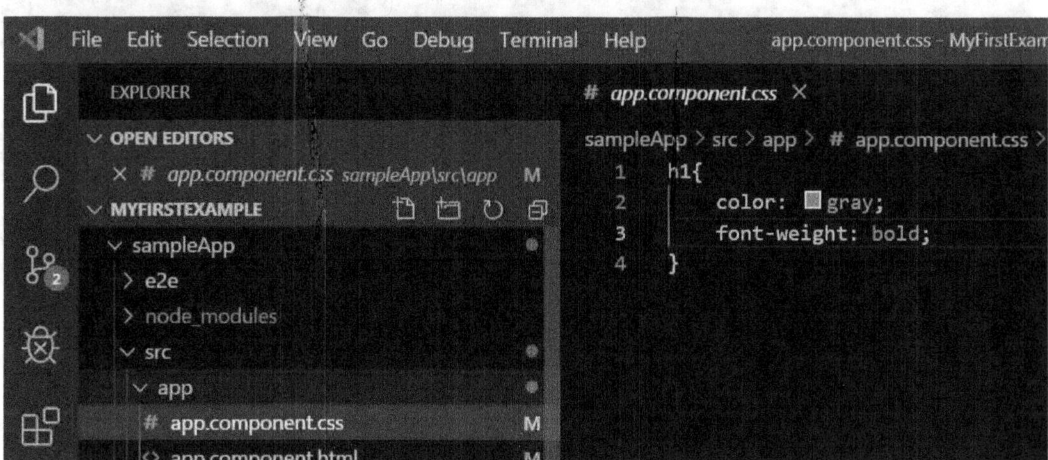

Running the application in the terminal displays output in the web browser as below.

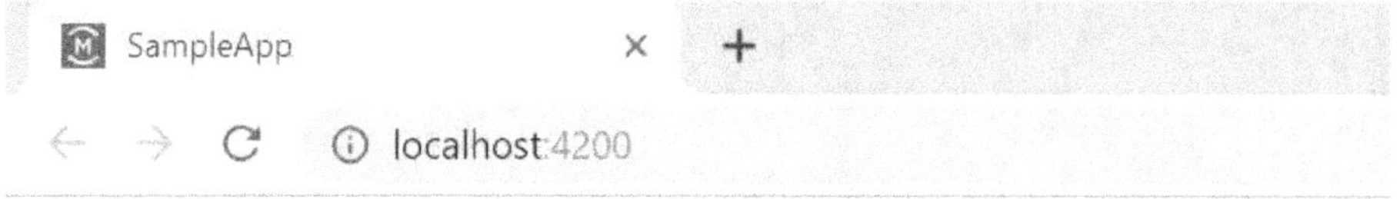

Hello Readers

IMPLEMENTING THE LOGIC

Most of the webpage backend processing logic in a web application is part of the component file. A root logic file 'app.component.ts', is created by default with ng new command. Use typescript to add logic to the required web pages in the application. Angular developers should have a basic understanding of JavaScript and typescript to expertise in this logic development phase.

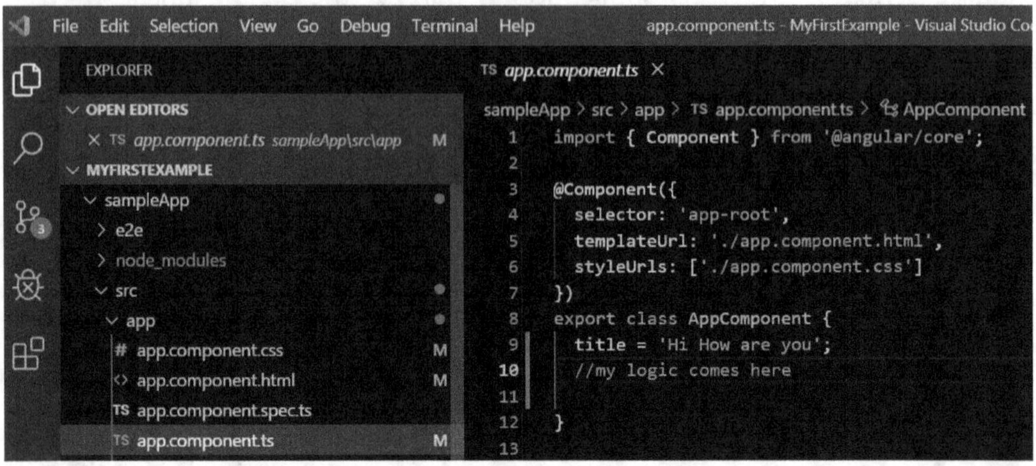

```typescript
1    import { Component } from '@angular/core';
2
3    @Component({
4      selector: 'app-root',
5      templateUrl: './app.component.html',
6      styleUrls: ['./app.component.css']
7    })
8    export class AppComponent {
9      title = 'Hi How are you';
10     //my logic comes here
11
12   }
13
```

Working with Objects

Targets for this Hour

- Creating an Object
- Displaying the Object Info
- Styling the Object Info

CREATING AN OBJECT

The object is the heart of the application development. Any technology, any programming language, or any framework, the developer must always start the thoughts towards the object, object, and object. Most of the core programming revolves around the object. A web developer should have a basic understanding of how the object looks like, how to write code related to the object.

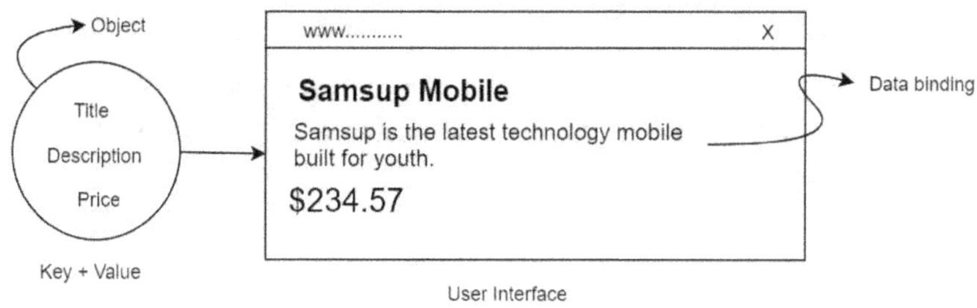

User Interface

In this section, the focus is on understand creating objects with simple examples. For example, a developer's task is to create a login page. The initial thought should be on how to create an object. To create an object, the developer should analyze what properties may be part of the object. In this case, the login screen requires properties username, password.

Below is how the UserLogin object looks with properties and sample values.

```
UserLogin = {
    UserName:'abc',
    Password:'def'
}
```

```
export class AppComponent {

    UserLogin:any = {
        UserName:'abc',
        Password:'def'
    }

}
```

The user login object '**UserLogin**' resides inside the component code.

```
1   import { Component } from '@angular/core';
2
3   @Component({
4     selector: 'app-root',
5     templateUrl: './app.component.html',
6     styleUrls: ['./app.component.css']
7   })
8   export class AppComponent {
9
10      UserLogin = {
11          UserName:'abc',
12          Password:'def'
13      }
14  }
```

With all the experience gained on creating user login objects, try creating a simple email object. Decide on a few properties which make sense for email like 'from', 'to', 'subject'. Create a 'ZeeMail' object with type 'any' as below.

```
1    import { Component } from '@angular/core';
2
3    @Component({
4      selector: 'app-root',
5      templateUrl: './app.component.html',
6      styleUrls: ['./app.component.css']
7    })
8    export class AppComponent {
9
10     ZeeMail:any = {
11         From:'parthav@gmail.com',
12         To:'asrith@gmail.com',
13         ReceivedTime:'10/10/2019',
14         Subject:'Hello How Are You',
15         Body: 'This is a sample email'
16     }
17   }
```

To get a complete grip on creating objects, try creating one more object for practice. This time focus is on creating a product object which may be part of the online shopping application.

```
1    import { Component } from '@angular/core';
2
3    @Component({
4      selector: 'app-root',
5      templateUrl: './app.component.html',
6      styleUrls: ['./app.component.css']
7    })
8    export class AppComponent {
9
10     MeeBayProduct:any = {
11         Title:'99 inches flat tv',
12         Price:'$230',
13         Description:'Nice and flat TV on deal only today',
14     }
15
16   }
```

DISPLAYING THE OBJECT INFO

Creating an object is fun. Creating an object is the first core part of the application development, whereas displaying the created object info on UI is the next phase of it. Use Angular interpolation {{ }} to display object info on the UI. Use the above-created object examples and display object info on the UI.

Write code to display the product object information on the UI. The code should be part of the components corresponding HTML file. To display object property value on the user interface, use 'ObjectName.PropertyName' inside double curly braces. In the example below Object name is 'MeeBayProduct', and the properties names are 'Title', 'Price', 'Description'.

```
1    import { Component } from '@angular/core';
2
3    @Component({
4      selector: 'app-root',
5      templateUrl: './app.component.html',
6      styleUrls: ['./app.component.css']
7    })
8    export class AppComponent {
9
10     MeeBayProduct:any = {
11         Title:'99 inches flat tv',
12         Price:'$230',
13         Description:'Nice and flat TV on deal only today',
14     }
15
16   }
```

Add interpolation in the UI code in app.component.html as below. '<br>' tag is used to add a line break between each displayed value.

```
TS app.component.ts ●      <> app.component.html ✕

firstexample > src > app > <> app.component.html > ...
1    {{MeeBayProduct.Title}}
2
3    <br>
4
5    {{MeeBayProduct.Description}}
6
7    <br>
8
9    {{MeeBayProduct.Price}}
```

Output in the browser looks like the below.

99 inches flat tv
Nice and flat TV on deal only today
$230

STYLING THE OBJECT INFO

To make the web page looks clean and stylish, the developer must apply styles to the displayed object info on the UI. The next step is to add styles to the above examples. As declared in the below screenshot, add three simple CSS classes to the HTML code.

```
TS app.component.ts ●      <> app.component.html ✕

firstexample > src > app > <> app.component.html > div.price
1    <div class="title">{{MeeBayProduct.Title}}</div>
2
3    <div class="desc">{{MeeBayProduct.Description}}</div>
4
5    <div class="price">{{MeeBayProduct.Price}}</div>
```

Add sample styles as below to the corresponding CSS file.

```
TS app.component.ts ●    <> app.component.html      # app.component.css ✕

firstexample > src > app > # app.component.css > .price
1    .title{
2      font-size: 30px;
3    }
4
5    .desc{
6    font-size: 16px;
7    }
8
9    .price{
10   font-size: 50px;
11   color: green;
12   }
```

After applying styles, output in the browser looks like the below.

99 inches flat tv

Nice and flat TV on deal only today

$230

Working with Lists

Targets for this Hour

- Creating Lists
- Displaying the List Information
- Styling a List
- Looping Through the List

CREATING A LIST

In the previous chapter, the focus is on creating objects. A list is an array of one or more objects. In simple terms, a list is an array of objects.

User Interface

Based on the above-created objects, the next step is to create lists using them.

```
 8    export class AppComponent {
 9
10      MeeBayProducts: any = [
11        {
12          Title: '99 inches flat tv',
13          Price: '$230',
14          Description: 'Nice and flat TV on deal only today',
15        },
16
17        {
18          Title: '32 inch smart phone',
19          Price: '$530',
20          Description: 'Smartest smart mobile ever',
21        }
22      ]
23
24    }
```

In layman's way of explanation, a list is a set of objects separated by commas in an array []. In the above example, a list 'meeBayProducts' is added using product objects in an array.

DISPLAYING THE LIST INFO

Use Angular interpolation {{ }} to display list info on the User Interface. One can also use a for loop to display list items if required. The next step is to consider an example of the above 'meeBayProducts' list, understand how to display list info on the UI.

Use the index to display list item content as below. List with the Index value displays an item in the list at that index instead of displaying the complete list. To pull the first item details from the list, use [o] index as below. Add CSS classes to the list items to improve the look and feel of the output. As explained in the previous chapter, take three CSS classes 'title', 'desc', 'price', and assign them to list items div.

```
TS app.component.ts        <> app.component.html  X      # app.component.css

firstexample > src > app > <> app.component.html > @ div.price
  1    <div class="title">{{MeeBayProducts[0].Title}}</div>
  2
  3    <div class="desc">{{MeeBayProducts[0].Description}}</div>
  4
  5    <div class="price">{{MeeBayProducts[0].Price}}</div>
```

Run the application in the terminal, view the output in the browser as below.

Using indexes 0 and 1, Display product list with first and second records. The HTML tag '<hr>' displays a line in between the two records.

```
TS app.component.ts        <> app.component.html  X      # app.component.css

firstexample > src > app > <> app.component.html > @ div.price
  1    <div class="title">{{MeeBayProducts[0].Title}}</div>
  2
  3    <div class="desc">{{MeeBayProducts[0].Description}}</div>
  4
  5    <div class="price">{{MeeBayProducts[0].Price}}</div>
  6
  7    <hr>
  8
  9    <div class="title">{{MeeBayProducts[1].Title}}</div>
 10
 11    <div class="desc">{{MeeBayProducts[1].Description}}</div>
 12
 13    <div class="price">{{MeeBayProducts[1].Price}}</div>
```

View the output displayed in the browser with first and second records.

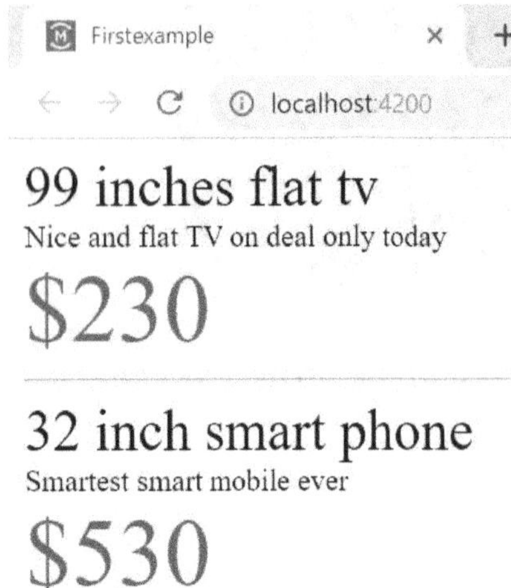

USING A FOR LOOP TO LOOP THROUGH THE LIST

It is a best practice to use a for loop instead of indexing array to display required list items info on the UI. The next step is to apply a for loop to display items from the above-defined list.

```
firstexample > src > app > app.component.html > div > div.price
1    <div *ngFor="let item of MeeBayProducts">
2
3        <div class="title">{{item.Title}}</div>
4        <div class="desc">{{item.Description}}</div>
5        <div class="price">{{item.Price}}</div>
6
7    </div>
```

To use 'for loop' in Angular, use '*ngFor' syntax. In the above example 'item' in 'let item of list'' syntax, 'item' holds the object values in each loop instance.

View the output displayed in the browser as below.

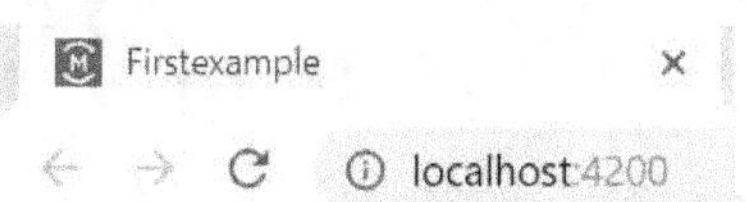

99 inches flat tv

Nice and flat TV on deal only today

$230

32 inch smart phone

Smartest smart mobile ever

$530

Functions and Events

Targets for this Hour

- Creating Functions
- Working with Events
- Calling Functions

CREATING FUNCTIONS

The component file holds most of the business logic for the web application. A function contains the reusable part of the code. Developers write one or more functions inside a component file.

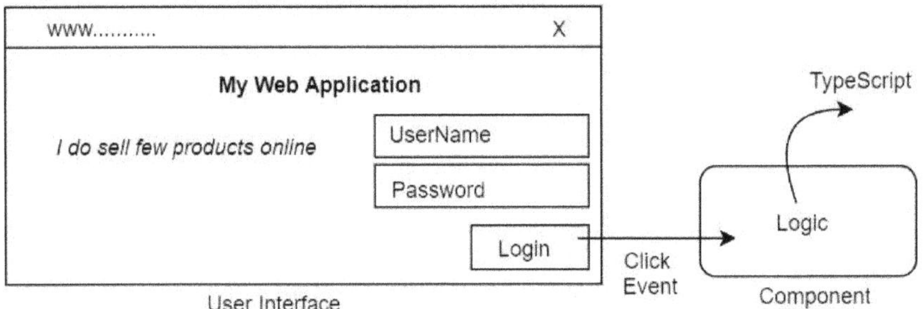

Consider creating a simple function that displays a simple alert inside the component file.

```
TS app.component.ts  X      <> app.component.html       # app

firstexample > src > app > TS app.component.ts > ...
  1    import { Component } from '@angular/core';
  2
  3    @Component({
  4      selector: 'app-root',
  5      templateUrl: './app.component.html',
  6      styleUrls: ['./app.component.css']
  7    })
  8    export class AppComponent {
  9
 10      testFunction() {
 11        alert('test');
 12      }
 13
 14    }
```

In the example above, the focus is on creating a simple function with the name 'testFunction'. The code related to the logic resides inside the function. In the example below, the focus is on adding simple logic to display an alert message.

The above code can be taken as a reference to create one or more functions similar to this function inside one or more component files in the Angular application.

WORKING WITH EVENTS

Actions on top of controls on the web page trigger via events. Consider a scenario where a button exists on the web page. The next step is to invoke some actions on the button. To perform one or more actions, use events. For example, handle click events using the syntax (click). Handling other events like 'mouseover' is similar.

CALLING FUNCTIONS

Calling functions inside the component from the HTML file achieved by just calling the function with the event. The below example uses the 'click' event. When the end-user clicks on the button, it fires the 'testFunction'. The next step is to focus on an example to handle a 'click' event in an Angular application.

```
TS app.component.ts  ✕        <> app.component.html  ✕

firstexample > src > app > <> app.component.html > ...
    1     <button (click)="testFunction()">
    2
    3       Click Me
    4
    5     </button>
```

In the example above, code in 'app.component.html' has an HTML button with the text 'Click Me'. In many generic scenarios in the web application, once a user clicks on the button, some logic should be triggered. The next step is to use a click event in the HTML file to call a function in the component file. In this case, write the business logic inside the 'testFunction' in the component file. Invoke the 'testFunction()' using (click) event.

Use the command 'ng serve –open' in the terminal to view the output in the browser for the above example. The web browser displays the output with a button. When a user clicks on the button, the application invokes '(click)' event, calls 'testFunction()', and then executes the business logic written inside the 'testFunction()' in the component file.

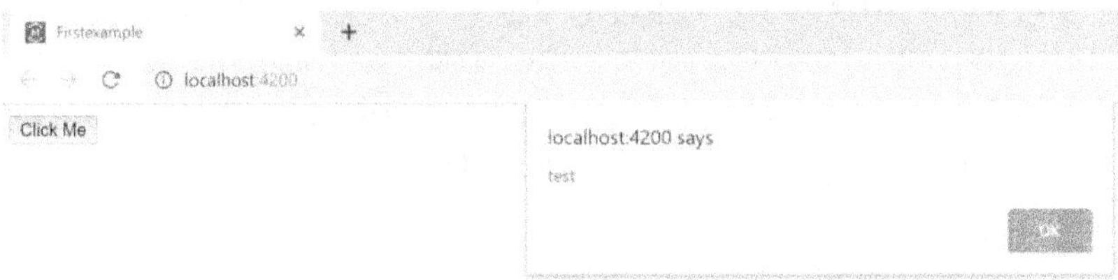

Extend the above example with some simple additional logic. Create a variable and display that variable value in the alert. The variable inside the component file should have a specific datatype. The declared variable can be called inside functions using 'this.VariableName'.

```ts
TS app.component.ts ×      <> app.component.html        #

firstexample > src > app > TS app.component.ts > ...
   1    import { Component } from '@angular/cor
   2
   3    @Component({
   4      selector: 'app-root',
   5      templateUrl: './app.component.html',
   6      styleUrls: ['./app.component.css']
   7    })
   8    export class AppComponent {
   9      i:any =10;
  10
  11      testFunction() {
  12        alert(this.i);
  13      }
  14
  15    }
```

In the above example, declare and assign a variable as 'i:any=10.' Call the declared variable using 'this.i' in the function.

Once the developer runs the application in the terminal, a button appears on the webpage as output. Clicking on the button displays the output with an alert in the browser as below.

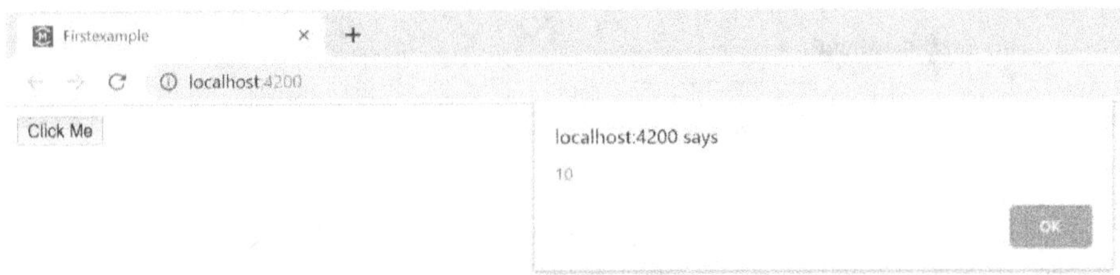

Working with Forms

In This Chapter Target

- Creating Forms
- Passing Values from UI to The Component
- Passing Values from The Component to the UI
- Importing Forms Module

One of the core areas in web application development is passing data between different layers in the application. During the Angular application development, the developer goes through many scenarios related to data passing between UI and business Logic and vice versa. In an Angular application, component holds most of the business logic.

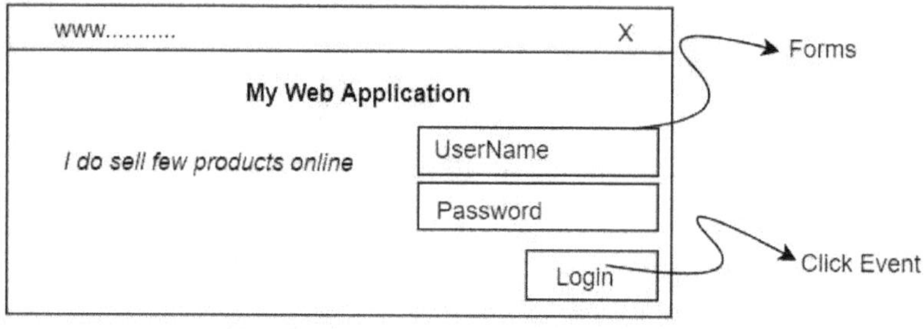

User Interface

PASSING VALUES FROM UI TO THE COMPONENT

The first step is to analyze the forms strategy using a simple form example. Create a form on the user interface and enter some values in the form controls.

In this example, the target is to read the entered values in the form, use them in the component. This UI-to-Component value passing strategy implementation involves using 'ngModel'. The syntax for using ngModel is '[(ngModel)]=name'. The next step is to implement 'ngModel' through a simple multiplication application.

```
app.component.html X      TS app.component.ts
ifcondi > src > app > <> app.component.html > ...
1    <input type="text" [(ngModel)] = "num1">
2    <input type="text" [(ngModel)] = "num2">
3
4    <button (click) = check()>Multiply</button>
5
6    <h1>
7        {{res}}
8    </h1>
```

In the below multiplication example, the user entered numbers are num1, num2. These are captured using ngModel and used as 'this.num1', 'this.num2' inside the component file.

```
8     export class AppComponent {
9         public num1: number = 0;
10        public num2: number = 0;
11        public res: number;
12
13        check() {
14            this.res = this.num1 * this.num2;
15            alert(this.res);
16        }
17    }
```

Once values are pulled from UI to the component, by using these values, business logic can be implemented based on the requirement. If the user must multiply, then the simple logic is to use (this.num1*this.num2) as a result. In the above multiplication example, initialize values to zero, and the variable 'res' holds the saved result.

PASSING VALUES FROM COMPONENT TO THE UI

Variables used in the component file can be used in the corresponding HTML file using double curly braces as below. In the above example, variable 'res' holds the result of the multiplication inside the component. Variable 'res' can be used inside double curly braces in the related HTML file as below to display the result in the browser.

```
6    <h1>
7        {{res}}
8    </h1>
```

Below is the output based on line 15 in 'app.component.ts'

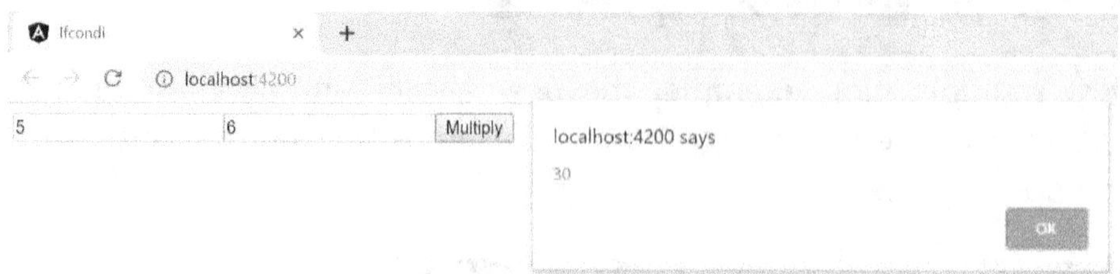

Below is the output based on line 14 in 'app.component.ts'.

30

CONFIGURING THE FORMS MODULE

To work on forms, import forms module inside the app module file. To do this, the developer should follow the two steps stated below. Adding these two steps is a onetime process. Verify if these two steps are already part of the module file before adding them. Missing these steps result in an error when working on forms development in an Angular application.

1. Import "FormsModule" from '@Angular/forms'.
2. Add the "FormsModule" to the import section in the "app.module.ts" file.

```
import { BrowserModule } from '@angular/platform-browser';
import { NgModule } from '@angular/core';

import { AppRoutingModule } from './app-routing.module';
import { AppComponent } from './app.component';
import { FormsModule } from '@angular/forms';

@NgModule({
  declarations: [
    AppComponent
  ],
  imports: [
    BrowserModule,
    AppRoutingModule,
    FormsModule
  ],
  providers: [],
  bootstrap: [AppComponent]
})
export class AppModule { }
```

Conditions

Targets for this Hour

- Where to Use Conditions
- How to Use If Condition

WHERE TO USE CONDITIONS

The usage of conditions plays a critical role in logic implementation during Angular application development. Conditions usage in Angular development applies to both components code as well as in the UI code.

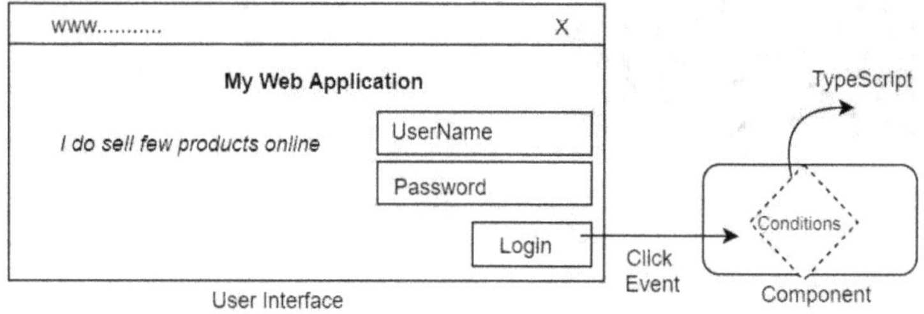

USING IF CONDITION

In Html code, the 'if' condition is used by '*ngIf=conditioncode' inside the HTML tag. The same 'if' condition can be used in component code as well using 'if{ code } else{ code }'. Use the same multiplication application with an if-else condition in component code to understand more about using conditions in Angular.

The example below demonstrates displaying a value based on a condition. If the multiplication result is greater than 100, then display one alert else display another alert. The 'res' variable holds the values of the result during the condition check. This res value is finally displayed in the alert on the browser, based on the condition.

```typescript
import { Component } from '@angular/core';

@Component({
  selector: 'app-root',
  templateUrl: './app.component.html',
  styleUrls: ['./app.component.css']
})
export class AppComponent {
  public num1: number = 0;
  public num2: number = 0;
  public res: string;

  check() {
    if (this.num1 * this.num2 > 100) {
      this.res = "greater than 100"
    } else {
      this.res = "not greater than 100"
    }

    alert(this.res);
  }
}
```

Output in the browser looks like the below if the result is greater than 100.

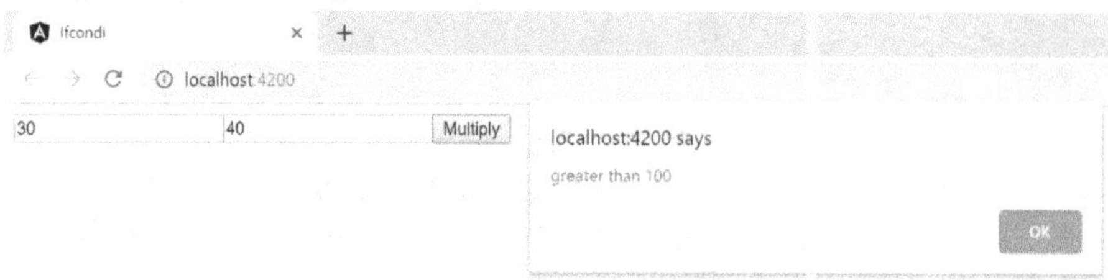

If the result is less than 100, output in the browser is an **alert displaying 'not greater than 100'**. Use **double curly braces to display 'res' value**. The browser displays the result as below.

not greater than 100

It is mandatory adding 'FormsModule' to the 'app.module.ts' file, as discussed in the previous chapter when working on forms-based code development.

```typescript
import { BrowserModule } from '@angular/platform-browser';
import { NgModule } from '@angular/core';

import { AppRoutingModule } from './app-routing.module';
import { AppComponent } from './app.component';
import { FormsModule } from '@angular/forms';

@NgModule({
  declarations: [
    AppComponent
  ],
  imports: [
    BrowserModule,
    AppRoutingModule,
    FormsModule
  ],
  providers: [],
  bootstrap: [AppComponent]
})
export class AppModule { }
```

Filtering Data

Targets for this Hour

- How to Filter The Data
- Filtering Scenarios

FILTERING SCENARIOS

Web application developers come across different scenarios where they write code to display a list of items data on the web page. This list of items data can be pulled from the database directly or pulled from the API. Few scenarios involve displaying a complete list of data. Many scenarios involve displaying filtered data instead of displaying complete data. Analyze this scenario by using a real live example. In a typical online shopping web application, the products page displays a list of products. Users have an option to search for products by typing the product name in the search box. Once the user enters the search keyword, clicks on the search or related button, then the filtered data is displayed on the page. Filtering data plays a significant role while writing business logic during Angular application development.

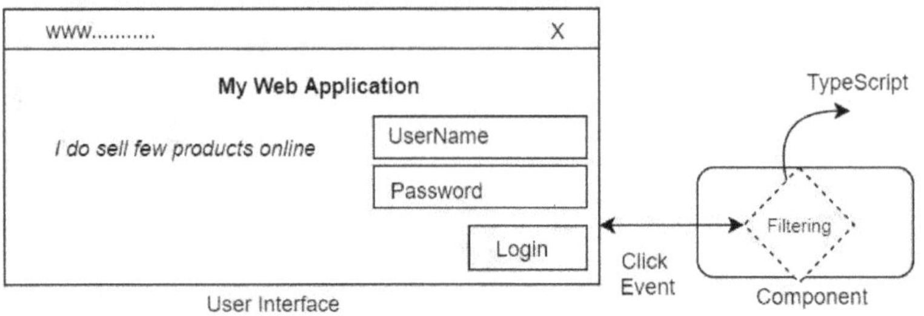

HOW TO FILTER DATA

To filter data, append a '.filter' syntax to the original list of items. Use an arrow function with a search string with the filter to get a list of filtered items based on the search key.

Consider creating a simple search application. From UI end, create a search text box, display a list of items below it. Once the user types the search string, clicks on the button, it should show the filtered results. Instead of a real database or API, consider working on a sample list of items. When the developer works on a live web application, this list of items may come from the database or API in many scenarios.

The first step is to add an HTML file with a plain textbox. Pass data from UI to the component using forms. To pass data from UI to Component, use 'ngModel', as discussed in the previous chapter. When the user clicks on the 'Search Now' button, then the button click event should fire. Once the event fires, call a function to implement the filter logic inside the component.

```
TS app.component.ts          <> app.component.html X      TS app.module.ts

testFiltering > src > app > <> app.component.html > button
  1    <input type="text" [(ngModel)]="searchKey">
  2    <button (click)="showResults()">Search Now</button>
```

In the below example, the focus is on creating a list named 'ZoogleData' and assigning data type any to it.

```
TS app.component.ts  ✕      <> app.component.html      TS app.module.ts

testFiltering > src > app > TS app.component.ts > ⌬ AppComponent
  8   export class AppComponent {
  9
 10     zoogleData:any = [
 11       {
 12         title:'what is hyderabad',
 13         shortDesc: 'hyderabad is a city'
 14       },
 15       {
 16         title:'infor about Chennai',
 17         shortDesc: 'Chennai is a city renamed from madras'
 18       },
 19       {
 20         title:'Who is Sharukh ',
 21         shortDesc: 'Sharukh is bollywood actor'
 22       },
 23       {
 24         title:'Who is pk',
 25         shortDesc: 'pawan kalyan is most popular, powerful Indian actor'
 26       },
 27     ]
 28
 29   }
```

Add sample titles and short descriptions added for each item in the list. Add a variable of type any to store the final filtered data. In the example, the variable to store final filtered data is 'filteredData'. The next step is to use a lambda expression like 'x=>x.title.includes("most"))'.

```
 11     zoogleData: any = [
 12       {
 13         title: 'what is hyderabad', shortDesc: 'hyderabad is a city'
 14       },
 15       {
 16         title: 'infor about Chennai', shortDesc: 'Chennai is a city renamed from madras'
 17       },
 18       {
 19         title: 'Who is Sharukh', shortDesc: 'Sharukh is bollywood actor'
 20       },
 21       {
 22         title: 'Who is pk', shortDesc: 'pawan kalyan is most popular, powerful Indian actor'
 23       },
 24     ]
 25     showResults() {
 26       this.filteredData = this.zoogleData.filter(p => p.shortDesc.includes("city"));
 27     }
 28   }
```

Hard code the short description filter to "city" and run the application. Adding this filter pulls records in the 'zoogleData' list, where the short description has the word "city" in it. Test the expected output in the browser. The next step is to remove the hardcoded value and place the real textbox value. 'this.searchKey" is the real value to use in this case.

```
21        {
22            title: 'Who is pk', shortDesc: 'pawan kalyan is most popular, powerful Indian actor'
23        },
24     ]
25     showResults() {
26         this.filteredData = this.zoogleData.filter(p => p.shortDesc.includes(this.searchKey));
27     }
28  }
```

Run the application in terminal using the command 'ng serve --open' to view output in the browser. Enter search string inside a text box as 'hyderabad,' and the developer should see only the results which contain the word 'hyderabad' in short description.

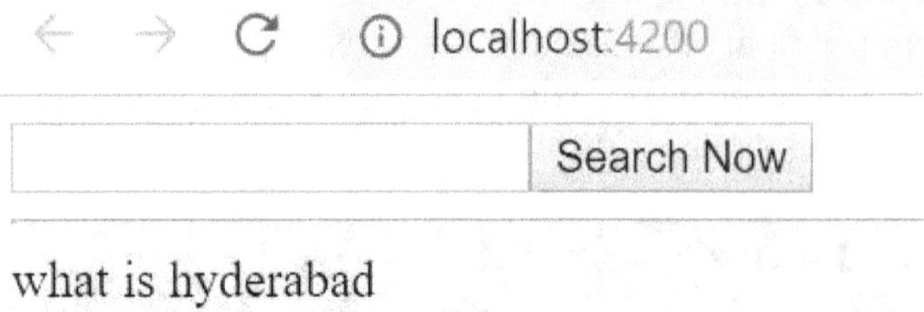

Go through the previous Lists chapter to understand how to loop through the list and display data on the web page using a 'for loop'.

It is mandatory to update the forms imports in the app module file, as discussed in the previous chapter when working with forms.

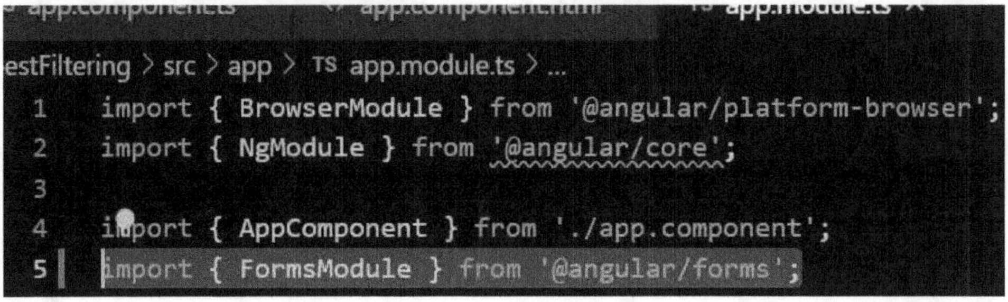

estFiltering > src > app > TS app.module.ts > ...

```typescript
1    import { BrowserModule } from '@angular/platform-browser';
2    import { NgModule } from '@angular/core';
3
4    import { AppComponent } from './app.component';
5    import { FormsModule } from '@angular/forms';
```

Classes

Targets for this Hour

- Creating a Class Inside, Outside the File
- Using a Class

CREATING A CLASS

The focus in the previous chapter was 'how to create an object', 'display the object info on the UI'. The keyword **'any'** is used as the data type for the Object. Based on the Angular expert's suggestions, the next step is to use classes instead of 'any' as part of the typescript code in Angular applications.

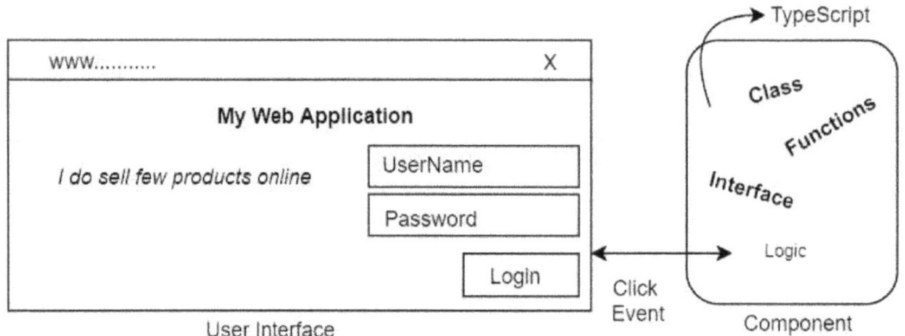

During the application execution, the typescript code compiles to JavaScript code behind the scenes.

```
export class AppComponent {

  details:any = {
      name: 'abc',
      phone:12,
      address:'hyd'
  };

}
```

As per standards, assigning data type **as** 'any' is not recommended. In this chapter, consider creating a class and replace it with type 'any'.

```
TS app.component.ts  ✕

testclass > src > app > TS app.component.ts > AppComponent
 1    import { Component } from '@angular/core';
 2
 3    @Component({
 4      selector: 'app-root',
 5      templateUrl: './app.component.html',
 6      styleUrls: ['./app.component.css']
 7    })
 8    export class AppComponent {
 9
10      details:any = {
11          name: 'abc',
12          phone:12,
13          address:'hyd'
14      };
15
16    }
```

Each class should have properties that are part of the class. Each property inside the class should have a related data type.

```
export class testing {
  name:string;
  phone:number;
  address:string;
}
```

Classes created should be exported and are used in other files by importing them. To export a class, prepend keyword 'export' to the class. Created classes can be part of the same file. In most cases, classes are separate files in the project. In the example below, create a class 'testing', as part of the 'details' object. As part of best practices, avoid using 'any' in all the cases.

```ts
TS app.component.ts  ✕

testclass > src > app > TS app.component.ts > ⚝ testing >
 1    import { Component } from '@angular/core'
 2
 3    @Component({
 4      selector: 'app-root',
 5      templateUrl: './app.component.html',
 6      styleUrls: ['./app.component.css']
 7    })
 8    export class AppComponent {
 9      title = 'testclass';
10      details:testing = {
11          name: 'abc',
12          phone:12,
13          address:'hyd'
14      };
15
16    }
17
18    export class testing {
19      name:string;
20      phone:number;
21      address:string;
22    }
23
```

CREATING A CLASS FILE

Classes can be part of the component file, or they can be a separate file. This section focuses on how to create a class as a separate file. To create a class file, use the command 'ng generate class classname'. In the example below, 'testing' is the new class name.

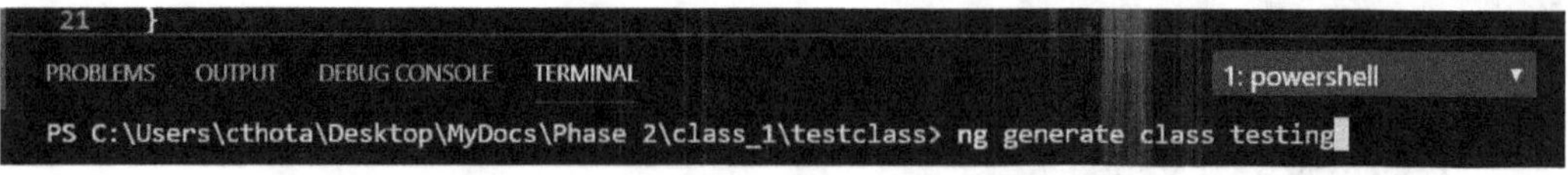

```
PROBLEMS   OUTPUT   DEBUG CONSOLE   TERMINAL                    1: powershell

PS C:\Users\cthota\Desktop\MyDocs\Phase 2\class_1\testclass> ng generate class testing
CREATE src/app/testing.spec.ts (158 bytes)
CREATE src/app/testing.ts (25 bytes)
PS C:\Users\cthota\Desktop\MyDocs\Phase 2\class_1\testclass>
```

IMPORTING THE CLASS

To the generated class file, add the required properties.

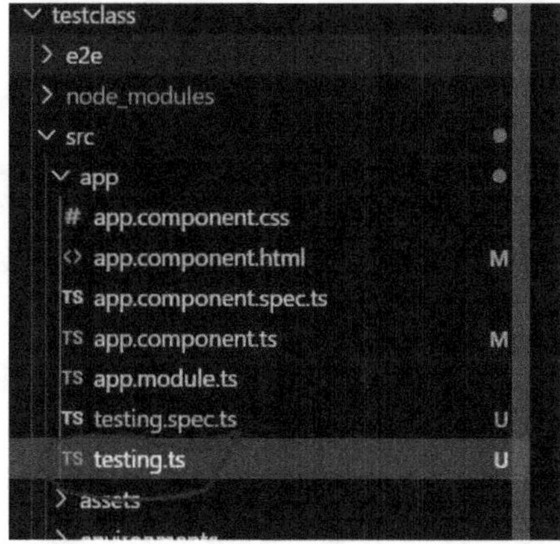

The class created can be imported by adding 'import {classname} from file path'.

USING A CLASS

To use a class inside the component file, import the class, and then assign the class to the variable. In the below example, the 'testing' class is created, imported, and then assigned it to variable 'details'.

```
TS app.component.ts  ✕      TS testing.ts

testclass > src > app > TS app.component.ts > ⚡ AppComponent
   1    import { Component } from '@angular/core';
   2    import { testing } from './testing';
   3
   4    @Component({
   5      selector: 'app-root',
   6      templateUrl: './app.component.html',
   7      styleUrls: ['./app.component.css']
   8    })
   9    export class AppComponent {
  10      title = 'testclass';
  11      details:testing = {
  12          name: 'abc',
  13          phone:12,
  14          address:'hyd'
  15      };
  16    }
```

Typescript playground utility available at the 'typescriptlang' website online gives us more details on how the compiled typescript code to JavaScript code looks. Create a few classes on the website and check the compiled JavaScript.

Interfaces

Targets for this Hour

- Creating an Interface Inside, Outside the File
- Using an Interface

Use Interfaces as part of the typescript code in Angular applications. Typescript code compiles to JavaScript code by the typescript compiler. In terms of converting typescript code to JavaScript, the typescript compiler does nothing in case of interfaces. It converts all other code to JavaScript except interface code. Interfaces are used only for type checking. Ignoring interfaces during compilation saves time, the burden on the application run time.

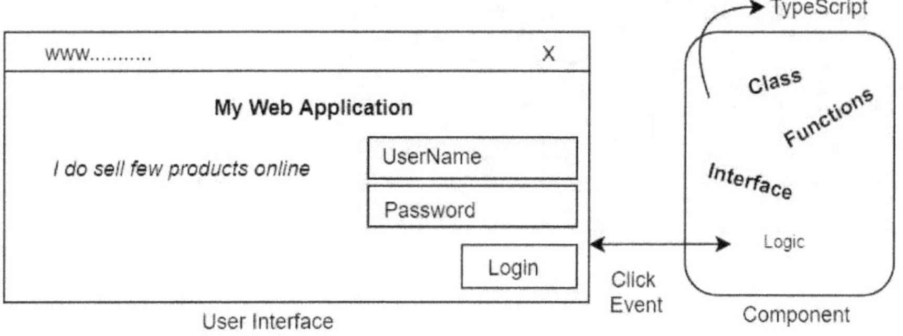

CREATING AN INTERFACE

Interfaces can be created inside the component or as a separate file. To create a new interface, use the command 'ng generate interface anyName' in the terminal and press the enter key. In the below example, create a new interface with the **name 'itesting'**.

Each Interface has properties that are part of the Interface. Creating an interface is like creating a class.

Each property inside the Interface should have a related data type.

IMPORTING AN INTERFACE

Interfaces created should be exported and are used in other files by importing them. To export an Interface, append 'export' to the Interface. Created Interfaces can be part of the same file. In most cases, Interfaces are separate files in the project. As part of best practice, avoid using 'any' in most of the cases.

```
TS app.component.ts  ✕      TS itesting.ts          TS testing.ts

testclass > src > app > TS app.component.ts > ⅏ AppComponent
  1    import { Component } from '@angular/core';
  2    import { Itesting } from './itesting';
  3
```

USING AN INTERFACE

To use an Interface inside the component file, import the Interface, and then assign the Interface to the variable. In the below example, create an Interface 'Itesting', imported class, and then assigned it to the **variable 'details'**.

```
TS app.component.ts  ✕      TS itesting.ts          TS testing.ts

testclass > src > app > TS app.component.ts > ⅏ AppComponent
  1    import { Component } from '@angular/core';
  2    import { Itesting } from './itesting';
  3
  4    @Component({
  5      selector: 'app-root',
  6      templateUrl: './app.component.html',
  7      styleUrls: ['./app.component.css']
  8    })
  9    export class AppComponent {
 10
 11      details:Itesting = {
 12        name: 'abc',
 13        phone:12,
 14        address:'hyd'
 15      };
 16    }
```

WHY AN INTERFACE AND A CLASS

As discussed above, the typescript compiler ignores interfaces and ignores converting them to JavaScript. Interfaces play a significant role where type checking is only required. Use classes in scenarios where developers need to instantiate objects with constructors, functional implementations.

Developing a website

Targets for this Hour

- Implementing Routing
- Creating Web Pages
- Linking Web Pages

IMPLEMENTING ROUTING

Code development until now focuses only on displaying results on a single web page. What if there are multiple web pages in the application? What if each page requires a separate logic and different styles for each page? In this context, use a concept called routing. Each page in the web application is related to one component.

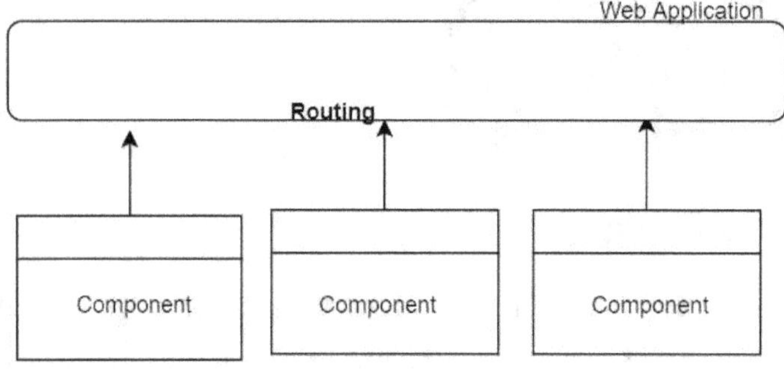

For example, if the developer plans to create a new web page, then a new component should be created. If the developer plans to create multiple web pages in the application, then multiple components should be created.

```
PROBLEMS   OUTPUT   DEBUG CONSOLE   TERMINAL                    1: powershell
PS C:\Users\cthota\Desktop\RoutingEx> ng new samplewebsite
```

While creating a new Angular application using the command 'ng new applicationName', the routing file is generated once the routing option is selected to 'Y'.

```
PROBLEMS   OUTPUT   DEBUG CONSOLE   TERMINAL

PS C:\Users\cthota\Desktop\RoutingEx> ng new samplewebsite
? Would you like to add Angular routing? (y/N) y
```

Implement routing in an "app-routing.module.ts" file.

```
v samplewebsite                          4
  > e2e                                  5       const routes: Routes = [];
  > node_modules                         6
  v src                                  7     @NgModule({
    v app                                8       imports: [RouterModule.forRoot(routes
      TS app-routing.module.ts           9       exports: [RouterModule]
      # app.component.css               10     })
      <> app.component.html             11     export class AppRoutingModule { }
      TS app.component.spec.ts          12
      TS app.component.ts
```

The first step before implementing routing is to make sure the developer creates a list of objects. Each object has components and path names information. Components are web page names, and pathnames are hyperlinks.

```
plewebsite > src > app > TS app-routing.module.ts > [∅] routes
    import { NgModule } from '@angular/core';
    import { Routes, RouterModule } from '@angular/router';



    const routes: Routes = [


    {path:'home',component:HomeComponent}


    ];
```

The below example demonstrates how to create a Routes list for a sample web application with few web pages. Create the routes list, import the related components.

```
TS app-routing.module.ts ✕

samplewebsite > src > app > TS app-routing.module.ts > ...
  1    import { NgModule } from '@angular/core';
  2    import { Routes, RouterModule } from '@angular/router';
  3    import { HomeComponent } from './home/home.component';
  4    import { AboutUsComponent } from './about-us/about-us.component';
  5    import { ContactUsComponent } from './contact-us/contact-us.component';
  6
  7
  8    const routes: Routes = [
  9
 10    {path:'home',component:HomeComponent},
 11    {path:'about',component:AboutUsComponent},
 12    {path:'contact',component:ContactUsComponent},
 13
 14    ];
```

CREATING WEB PAGES

Creating a web page for the web application means creating a component using CLI command 'ng generate component "component name" '.

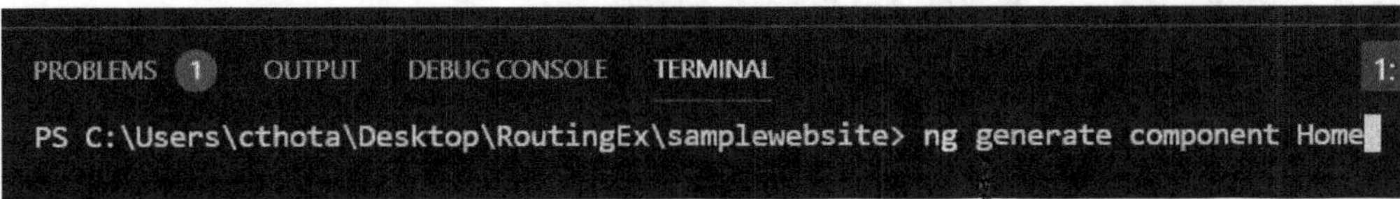

If the developer plan to develop multiple web pages for the web application, then use the same command multiple times with different component/web page names. Design, style, and add logic to the web pages as required. After adding the pages, make sure the routing file updates match the above explanation.

```
PROBLEMS 1    OUTPUT    DEBUG CONSOLE    TERMINAL    1: p
PS C:\Users\cthota\Desktop\RoutingEx\samplewebsite> ng generate component Home
CREATE src/app/home/home.component.html (19 bytes)
CREATE src/app/home/home.component.spec.ts (614 bytes)
CREATE src/app/home/home.component.ts (261 bytes)
CREATE src/app/home/home.component.css (0 bytes)
UPDATE src/app/app.module.ts (467 bytes)
PS C:\Users\cthota\Desktop\RoutingEx\samplewebsite> ng generate component AboutUs
```

```
PS C:\Users\cthota\Desktop\RoutingEx\samplewebsite> ng generate component ContactUs
CREATE src/app/contact-us/contact-us.component.html (25 bytes)
CREATE src/app/contact-us/contact-us.component.spec.ts (650 bytes)
CREATE src/app/contact-us/contact-us.component.ts (284 bytes)
CREATE src/app/contact-us/contact-us.component.css (0 bytes)
UPDATE src/app/app.module.ts (651 bytes)
```

LINKING WEB PAGES

Linking web pages is as simple as using an anchor tag. In Angular, use the router link attribute to link to related web pages.

For example, with this block of code '<a routerLink="/Contact">Contact Us</a>', when the user clicks on the 'Contact Us' link, then the user is redirected to component and web page developed for contact.

```
TS app-routing.module.ts      <> app.component.html  ×

samplewebsite > src > app > <> app.component.html > router-outlet
  1    <a routerLink="/Home">
  2      Home
  3    </a>  |
  4    <a routerLink="/About">
  5      About
  6    </a> |
  7
  8    <a routerLink="/Contact">
  9      Contact
 10    </a>
 11
 12
 13    <router-outlet></router-outlet>
```

Run the application using 'ng serve –open', and the output appears in the browser with links to all developed web pages.

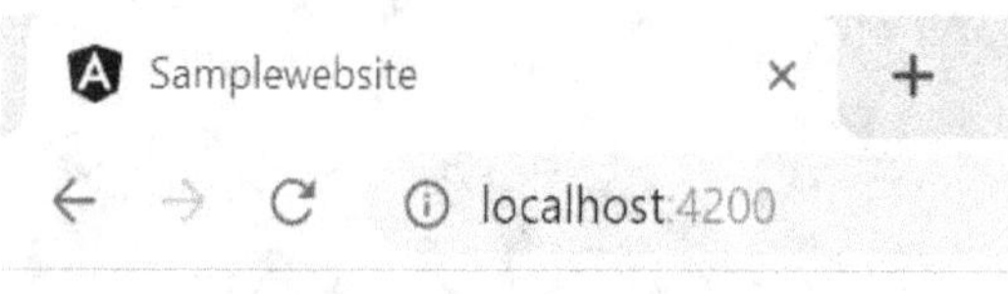

Open respective pages component.html to add design, CSS file to add styles, ts file to add logic to the application.

```
TS app-routing.module.ts      <> app.component.html      <> about-us.componen

samplewebsite > src > app > about-us > <> about-us.component.html > ...
  1    <p>I will add my about content here</p>
  2
```

To navigate to individual pages, use the router path in the URL based on the route file created above.

Home | About | Contact

I will add my about content here

To summarize, creating live web application involves
- Adding required routes to the routing file
- Creating Required web pages
- Linking web pages

Hour **15**

Visibility to the world

Targets for this Hour

- Creating Production Build
- Working With FTP
- Deploying Files to The Server

CREATING PRODUCTION BUILD

The web application created until now is on the local computer. The final goal is to make sure this web application is available and accessible across the world. Use a process called deployment to move files from local to a remote server. Indirectly moving the required files to a web server is called deployment.

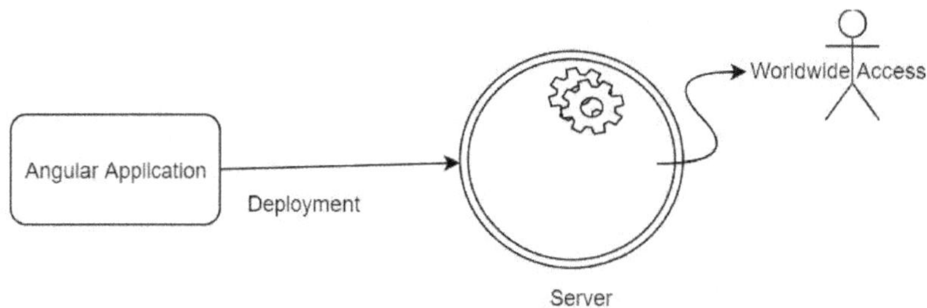

Even though there are multiple files in the application, not all files are required to move to the server. Few files can be compressed to one or more files to decrease the number of hits to the server. This compression process increases the performance of the application. The whole process of compression, creating files for production deployment, is done using the command 'ng build –prod'.

```
PROBLEMS   OUTPUT   DEBUG CONSOLE   TERMINAL

 PS C:\Users\cthota\Desktop\RoutingEx\samplewebsite> ng build --prod
```

The command execution generates a **folder called 'dist'** with few files. Dist folder contains required files and compressed files for deployment.

```
PROBLEMS   OUTPUT   DEBUG CONSOLE   TERMINAL                         1: powershell

4 unchanged chunks
chunk {main} main.js, main.js.map (main) 33.2 kB [initial] [rendered]
Time: 262ms
i ⎡wdm⎤: Compiled successfully.
i ⎡wdm⎤: Compiling...

Date: 2019-10-20T17:46:06.781Z - Hash: 2ee77cf4aa6e2edceb6d
4 unchanged chunks
chunk {main} main.js, main.js.map (main) 33.2 kB [initial] [rendered]
Time: 195ms
i ⎡wdm⎤: Compiled successfully.
PS C:\Users\cthota\Desktop\RoutingEx\samplewebsite> ng build --prod
Generating ES5 bundles for differential loading...
ES5 bundle generation complete.

chunk {0} runtime-es2015.e8a2810b3b08d6a1b6aa.js (runtime) 1.45 kB [entry] [rendered]
chunk {0} runtime-es5.e8a2810b3b08d6a1b6aa.js (runtime) 1.45 kB [entry] [rendered]
chunk {2} polyfills-es2015.0ef207fb7b4761464817.js (polyfills) 36.4 kB [initial] [rendered]
chunk {3} polyfills-es5.2b9ce34c123ac007a8ba.js (polyfills-es5) 122 kB [initial] [rendered]
chunk {1} main-es2015.76fe9d3f4309ac4d6296.js (main) 213 kB [initial] [rendered]
chunk {1} main-es5.76fe9d3f4309ac4d6296.js (main) 245 kB [initial] [rendered]
chunk {4} styles.3ff695c00d717f2d2a11.css (styles) 0 bytes [initial] [rendered]
Date: 2019-10-20T17:51:54.108Z - Hash: a368e672eef0753a4893 - Time: 23156ms
PS C:\Users\cthota\Desktop\RoutingEx\samplewebsite>
```

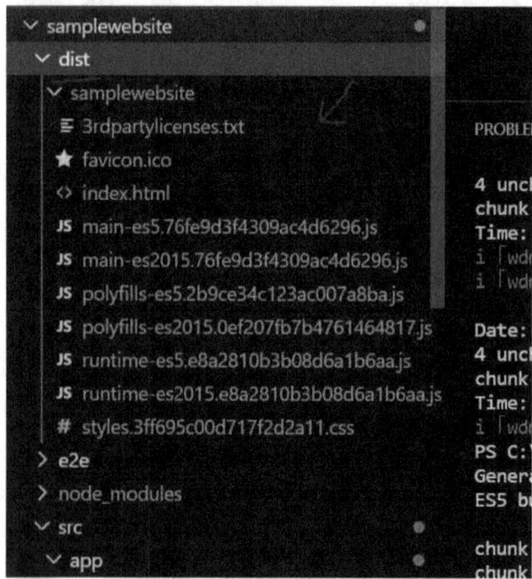

WORKING WITH FTP

To deploy files to the server, the developer should purchase a domain and hosting service. Once the developer purchases a domain and hosting from any service provider online, the developer gets an option to create an FTP user in the control panel provided by the service provider. The developer also gets the option to create an FTP username and password for the hosting server for file deployment. The following minimum details are required to move files to the FTP server.

1. **FTP server name**
2. **FTP username**
3. **FTP password**

If the developer has trouble in understanding the process of creating FTP details, then the developer can contact the service provider, where the domain and hosting are purchased, and the service provider can set up the FTP details.

DEPLOYING FILES TO THE SERVER

There are many ways to deploy the developed web application to servers. There are automated ways and manual ways to do it. Consider one manual process to understand some depth inside deployment. Once the developer has the required details to deploy required files, follow the below steps to deploy files to the live server.

1. Open Windows file explorer.
2. In the URL bar, Type FTP server name, press enter.
3. When it prompts to enter credentials, then enter username and password and press enter.
4. If the developer enters the correct credentials, it opens a folder.

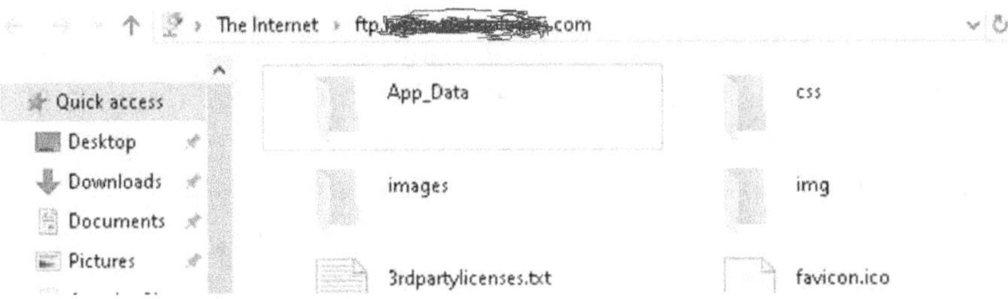

5. Right-click on the dist folder and select reveal in explorer.

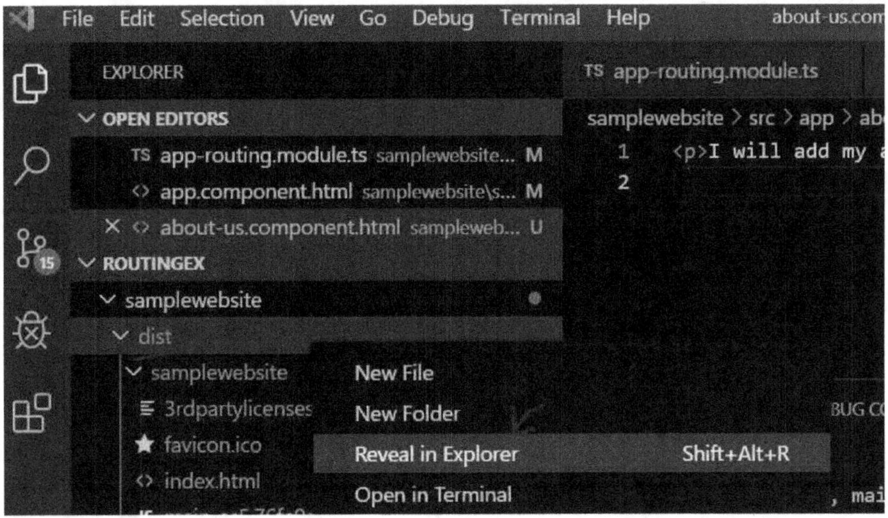

6. Selecting 'Reveal in Explorer' on the 'dist' folder displays all files which should be copied and pasted in the server.
7. Copy files from the 'dist' folder generated as a result of command 'ng build –prod'
8. Paste files in the required folder on the FTP server.

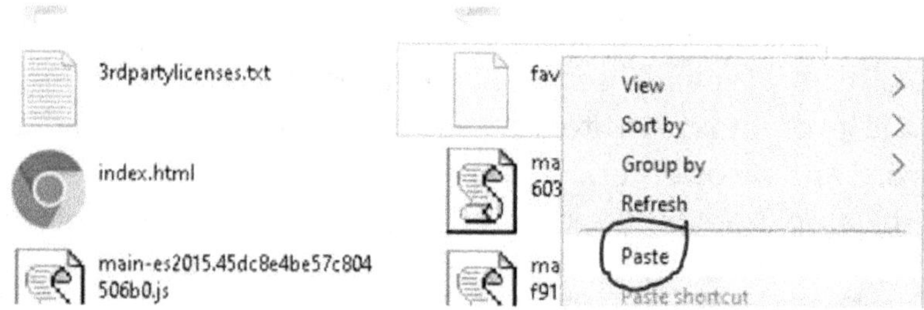

9. Confirming pasting all files to the server is considered deployment complete.
10. Validate the website after completing the deployment.

Services the Backbone

Targets for this Hour

- Why Services
- Creating Services
- Calling Services
- Module Updates

WHY SERVICES

Suppose an Angular application has multiple components. Assume many components use the same logic. Instead of writing the same logic numerous times in each component, one option is to create a service where the developer can write the common logic.

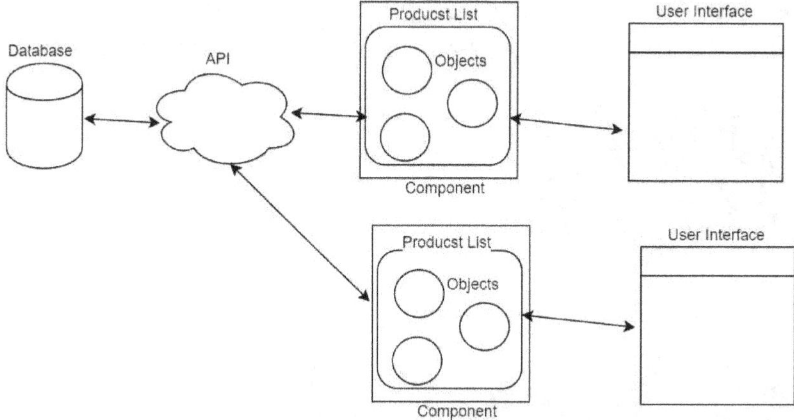

Each component in the application calls the service and use the common logic.

Services are beneficial in applications where multiple components share the same logic. Consider a simple product application as an example to explore services.

IMPLEMENTING COMMON LOGIC

The first step is to create a service and move the common logic to a service. Use the command 'ng new products' to create a new application. A minimum of two components and one service are required. The goal is to make the two components use the same service.

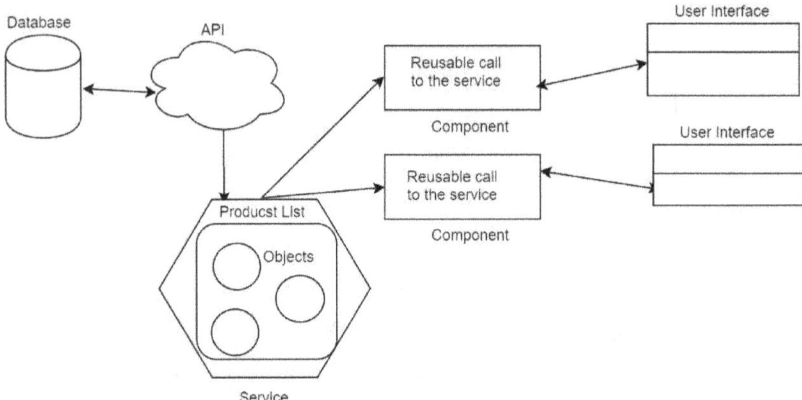

Use commands 'ng generate component page1', 'ng generate component page2' to create two web pages in the application. Consider taking two example products and display the first product on the user interface.

```
getFirstProduct() {
  this.products = ['TV', 'Mobile'];
  this.prod1 = this.products[0];
}
```

Use the 'prod1' variable to display the result on the UI.

```
products > src > app > page1 > <> page1.component.html
    1    {{prod1}}
```

Consider the scenario where the same logic should be used in other web pages also. The logic written on page 1 should also be part of page 2 to display data on the second page. One of the bad practices in web application development is code duplication. Multiple components should not have the same code.

```
TS page1.component.ts ×      TS page2.component.ts

products > src > app > page1 > TS page1.component.ts >
10        products: any;
11        prod1: any;
12
13        getFirstProduct() {
14            this.products = ['TV', 'Mobile'];
15            this.prod1 = this.products[0];
16        }
17
18        ngOnInit() {
19            this.getFirstProduct();
20        }
```

```
.component.ts      TS page2.component.ts ×      <> app.c

products > src > app > page2 > TS page2.component.ts >
12        products: any;
13        prod1: any;
14
15        getFirstProduct() {
16            this.products = ['TV', 'Mobile'];
17            this.prod1 = this.products[0];
18        }
19
20        ngOnInit() {
21            this.getFirstProduct();
22        }
```

Move all the common code to a service and use the service in all required components.

CALLING SERVICE FROM THE COMPONENT

To create a service, use the command 'ng generate service name'. In the example below, use the service name as 'getProductsName'. Move the code from component file to service file. Once moved, the logic required for both the component files points to the service.

```ts
TS page1.component.ts          TS getproducts.service.ts  X     TS

products > src > app > TS getproducts.service.ts > ...
  1    import { Injectable } from '@angular/core';
  2
  3    @Injectable({
  4      providedIn: 'root'
  5    })
  6    export class GetproductsService {
  7      products: any;
  8      prod1: any;
  9
 10      getFirstProduct() {
 11        this.products = ['TV', 'Mobile'];
 12        this.prod1 = this.products[0];
 13        return this.prod1;
 14      }
 15      constructor() { }
 16    }
 17
```

The next step is to write code to call service inside the component file. Import the service to the component.

```ts
TS page1.component.ts  X     TS getproducts.service.ts       TS page2.component.ts

products > src > app > page1 > TS page1.component.ts > ...
  1    import { Component, OnInit } from '@angular/core';
  2    import { GetproductsService } from '../getproducts.service';
  3
  4    @Component({
  5      selector: 'app-page1',
```

Declare the service variable inside the constructor.

```ts
export class Page1Component implements OnInit {

  constructor(private svc: GetproductsService) { }
```

Call the service method in any component with a variable created in the constructor. In the below example, the 'svc' is the variable to call service functions. The same procedure should be followed by any other component in the application to access the service.

```
ngOnInit() {
   this.prod1 = this.svc.getFirstProduct();
}
```

One final step is to Update the app.module.ts file to add the created service to provider array. Open file app.module.ts and add the service name to the provider array.

```
   BrowserModule
],
providers: [GetproductsService],
bootstrap: [AppComponent]
})
export class AppModule { }
```

Add the selector to the HTML code, run the application to display output on the browser.

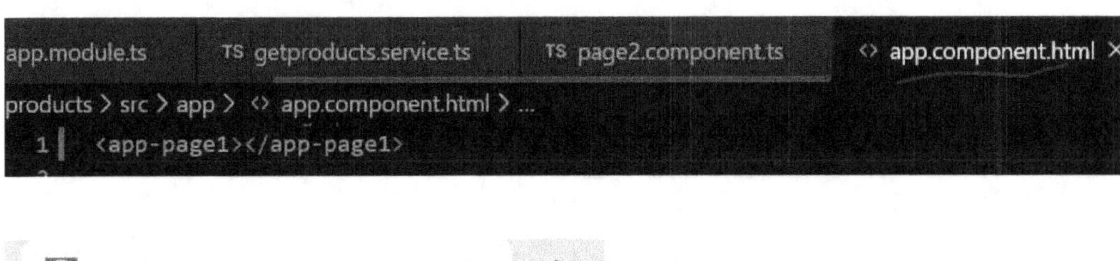

TV

Components Deep Dive

Targets for this Hour

- Creating Components
- Passing Parameters

CREATING COMPONENTS

The web application can have multiple web pages. Consider each web page as a component. Each component is a group of HTML, CSS, typescript, spec files. The example below demonstrates the student component.

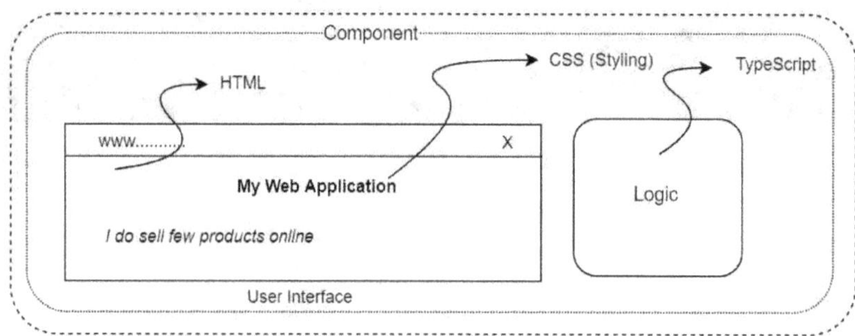

The first step is to generate a component using the command 'ng generate component name'.

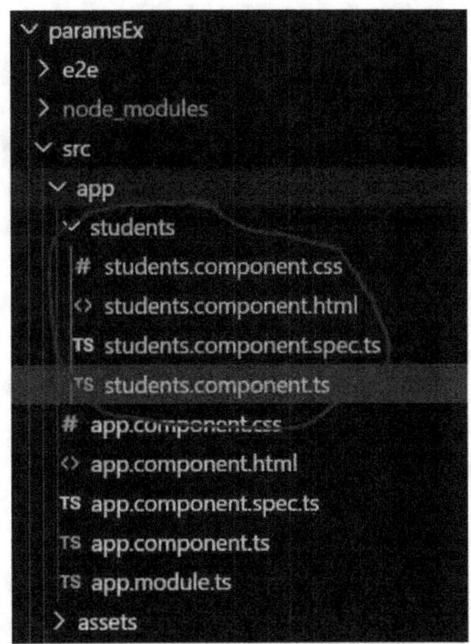

Each web page may also have one or more components in it. In general web applications, the developer usually creates components and reuse them on different web pages. As an Angular web developer, one should be very familiar with

1. How to create components
2. How to use components in the parent HTML file
3. Using the same component multiple times, with different parameters

To understand the above three items, **create a component 'student'** using the command **'ng generate component student'**. The student component adds HTML, CSS, ts, spec files.

```
∨ src
  ∨ app
    ∨ students
      #  students.component.css
      <> students.component.html
      TS students.component.spec.ts
      TS students.component.ts
```

The next step is to add the required logic to the component. Add a simple student object with name, address, and phone.

```
<> students.component.html        TS students.con
src > app > students > TS students.component.ts
 13
 14        constructor() {}
 15
 16        ngOnInit() {
 17          this.stud = {
 18            name: 'test name',
 19            address: 'test address',
 20            phone: 'test phone'
 21          };
 22        }
```

To display the student object info on the web page, use double curly braces with objects and property. Use the terminal to run the application and view student information on the web page.

```
<> students.component.html X    TS students.component.ts
src > app > students > <> students.component.html > ...
 1    <h1>{{stud.name}}</h1>
 2    <h2>{{stud.address}}</h2>
 3    <h3>{{stud.phone}}</h3>
 4
```

Run the application in the terminal, and the webpage displays the output as below. Adding the selector to parent HTML file 'app.component.html' displays output with that component output.

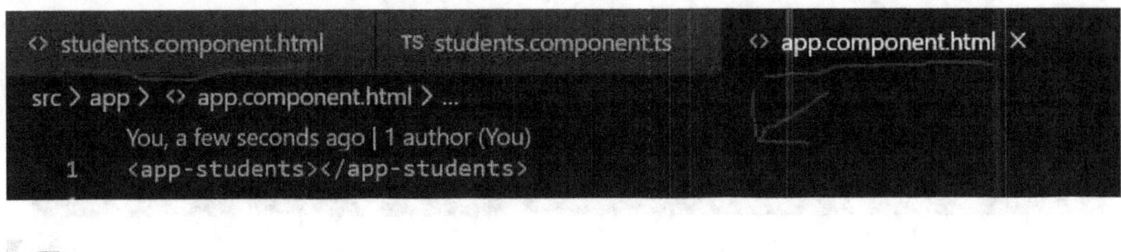

PASSING PARAMETERS

Create a student component, and the developer can use the same student component selector in multiple files. At the same time, the developer can use the same component with different parameters. To accept the parameter, use the '@Input(property) variable' in the class.

```ts
TS students.component.ts  X

paramsEx > src > app > students > TS students.component.ts > StudentsCompor
1    import { Component, OnInit, Input } from '@angular/core';
2
3    @Component({
4      selector: 'app-students',
5      templateUrl: './students.component.html',
6      styleUrls: ['./students.component.css']
7    })
8    export class StudentsComponent implements OnInit {
9      stud: any
10     @Input('name') username:any;
11     @Input('address') address:any;
12     @Input('phone') phone:any;
```

Use selectors in HTML any number of times, pass the parameters as below example.

```
<> app.component.html  X

paramsEx > src > app > <> app.component.html > ⊘ app-students
  1    <app-students name="chandra1" phone="123" address="hyd"></app-students>
  2    <app-students name="chandra2" phone="456" address="secbad"></app-students>
  3    <app-students name="chandra3" phone="789" address="warangal"></app-students>
```

Use this.property in the student component to read the parameter.

```
<> students.component.html  X        TS students.component.ts  X

src > app > students > TS students.component.ts > ⅏ StudentsC
  15
  16        ngOnInit() {
  17          this.stud = {
  18            name: this.username,
  19            address: this.address,
  20            phone: this.phone
  21          };
  22        }
```

Run the application to see the same component values with different parameters on the browser.

ParamsEx

← → C ⓘ localhost:4200

chandra1

hyd

123

chandra2

secbad

456

chandra3

warangal

789

Using Directives

Targets for this Hour

- Why Directives
- Creating Directives

WHY DIRECTIVES

The document object model is modified using the directives. A few example scenarios where directives are used, including but not limited to, show, or hide some sections of the web page based on conditions, standard code to format an element of the webpage.

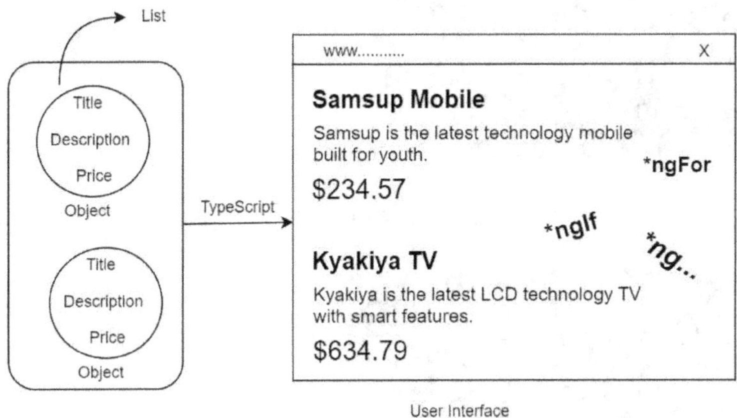

User Interface

There are two different types of directives in Angular. Built-in directive where developers can use the existing directives defined in Angular, custom directives where developers develop the directives from start to end. Built-in directives include

- o ngFor
- o ngIf
- o ngSwitchCase
- o ngClass
- o ngStyle

USING BUILT-IN DIRECTIVES

The initial step is to understand how to use a built-in directive in the application. Consider a simple scenario where some products exist in an array, and If products exist, **display 'Products found' else display 'no products found'** on the user interface. Use a built-in directive *ngIf to work on this scenario. In the example below, take an empty product array.

```
<> app.component.html          TS app.component.ts  X

simpleif > src > app > TS app.component.ts > ...
    3     @Component({
    4        selector: 'app-root',
    5        templateUrl: './app.component.html',
    6        styleUrls: ['./app.component.css']
    7     })
    8     export class AppComponent {
    9        products =[];
   10     }
```

Use *ngIf to check if products exist. Apply this logic to the HTML elements.

```
<> app.component.html  X          TS app.component.ts

simpleif > src > app > <> app.component.html > ...
    1  v <div *ngIf="products.length > 0">
    2        Products found
    3     </div>
```

```
<> app.component.html X        TS app.component.ts

simpleif > src > app > <> app.component.html > ...
  1  v <div *ngIf="products.length > 0">
  2         Products found
  3     </div>
  4
  5  v <div *ngIf="products.length == 0">
  6         Products not found
  7     </div>
```

Because of the empty product array, after the application execution in the terminal, the browser displays the output as 'products not found'.

Add one or more products to the product array to test the second element condition.

```
<> app.component.html X      TS app.component.ts X

simpleif > src > app > TS app.component.ts > ...
   3     @Component({
   4        selector: 'app-root',
   5        templateUrl: './app.component.html',
   6        styleUrls: ['./app.component.css']
   7     })
   8     export class AppComponent {
   9        products =['TV','Mobile'];
  10     }
```

Because of the nonempty product array, after the application execution in the terminal, the browser displays the output as 'products found'.

Products found

CREATING CUSTOM DIRECTIVES

The subsequent step is to create a custom directive and use it in one of the web pages created in the application. As an example scenario, create a simple directive that applies some style to the HTML element to which the directive is applied. Use the command 'ng generate directive name'. In the example below, 'abc' is the directive name. Use the command 'ng generate directive abc' to create a new custom directive. Executing the above command creates two files. One is a directive file, and the other one is a test file.

Open the directive file to view the selector name. This selector name is the final directive, which we apply to the required HTML elements. Apply the created directive to any number of HTML elements.

```
TS abc.directive.ts ×

sampleDirectiveApp > src > app > TS abc.directive.
  1     import { Directive, ElementRef,
  2
  3     @Directive({
  4       selector: '[appAbc]'
  5     })
  6     export class AbcDirective {
```

Add some simple code to the current HTML element 'this.elementRef', to apply colour and height.

```
TS abc.directive.ts ×

sampleDirectiveApp > src > app > TS abc.directive.ts > ᪽ AbcDirective > ⊘ ngOnInit
  1     import { Directive, ElementRef, OnInit } from '@angular/core';
  2
  3     @Directive({
  4       selector: '[appAbc]'
  5     })
  6     export class AbcDirective {
  7
  8       constructor(private elementRef: ElementRef) { }
  9       ngOnInit() {
 10         this.elementRef.nativeElement.style.backgroundColor = 'green';
 11         this.elementRef.nativeElement.style.height='200px';
 12       }
 13     }
```

Apply the directive to one HTML element as below. The element should get the directive logic applied.

```
<> app.component.html ×

sampleDirectiveApp > src > app > <> app
  1     <div appAbc>Hello</div>
```

Run the application in the terminal to view the output in the browser. The logic added to the directive applies to the element in the browser.

Working with Pipes

Targets for this Hour

- Why Pipes
- Built-In Pipes
- Creating Pipes

WHY PIPES

Pipes logically format the displaying value in the HTML. Use the symbol '|' as a pipe to change the value in HTML. With pipes usage, the actual value remains unchanged. Change is applied only to the value before displaying it on the browser.

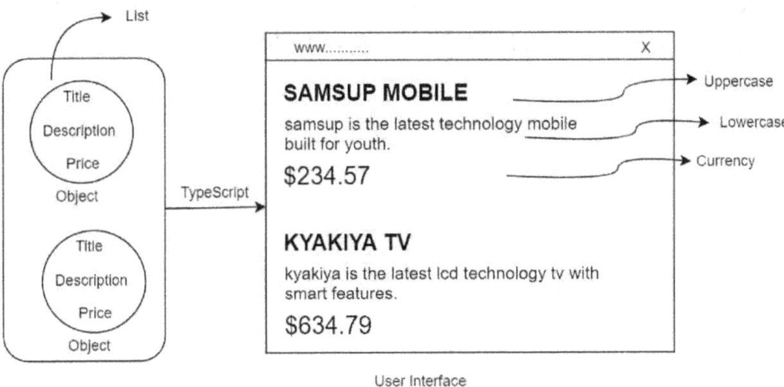

User Interface

There are two types of Pipes, which an Angular developer, use in application development. Inbuilt pipes are provided by Angular, and custom pipes, which developers should develop from the start and use it in different areas of the code.

BUILT-IN PIPES

Few built-in pipes that come with Angular are below. The name of the pipe is self-explanatory on the functionality it does.

- Lowercase
- Uppercase
- Percent
- Decimal
- Slice
- Date
- Currency
- JSON

USING BUILT-IN PIPES

The first step is to work on a simple example to understand how to use the pipe. Using an inbuilt 'lowercase' pipe, consider a sample scenario to convert a sentence from any case to lower case. In the example below, assign a sentence to a variable 'title'.

```
<> app.component.html          TS app.component.ts  X

pipeexmple > src > app > TS app.component.ts > AppCompor
  1    import { Component } from '@angular/core';
  2
  3    @Component({
  4      selector: 'app-root',
  5      templateUrl: './app.component.html',
  6      styleUrls: ['./app.component.css']
  7    })
  8    export class AppComponent {
  9
 10      title = 'Hello How ARE YoU';
 11
 12    }
```

Use the title in double curly braces with a lower-case pipe as below.

```
<> app.component.html  X    TS app.component.ts

pipeexmple > src > app > <> app.component.html > ...
  1
  2      <h1>
  3        {{title | lowercase}}
  4      </h1>
```

The browser displays output with the sentence in the lowercase. If required, use multiple pipes, one next to another, to the value through the process called chaining pipes.

hello how are you

CREATING CUSTOM PIPES

Occasionally, the built-in Angular pipes are not enough to perform an action based on the requirement for the application. Develop custom pipes in these scenarios. To create a custom pipe, use the command 'ng generate pipe anyname'.

In the example below, the command 'ng generate pipe abc' is used to create required pipe files. The logic related to the file is part of the typescript file. In this example, 'abc.pipe.ts' file holds the logic. To understand custom pipes with ease, create a straightforward pipe which multiples any given value with 100. When the developer applies an 'abc' pipe to any number in the HTML, the output on the browser displays number multiplied by 100.

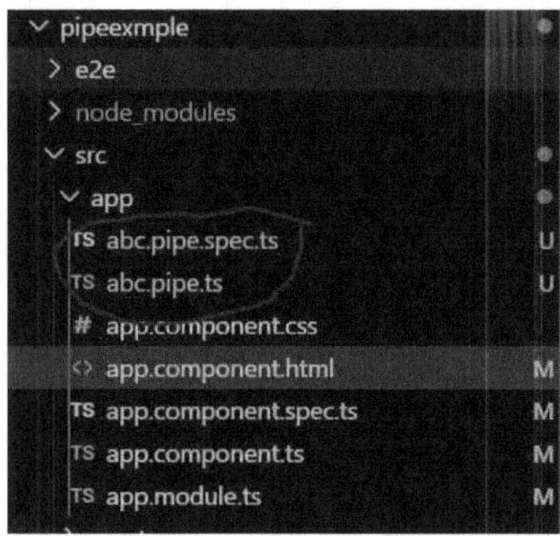

Use the pipe name with a pipe symbol next to the value in the HTML code.

```
<> app.component.html        TS abc.pipe.ts  X

pipeexmple > src > app > TS abc.pipe.ts > ...
   1    import { Pipe, PipeTransform } from '@angular/core';
   2
   3    @Pipe({
   4      name: 'abc'
   5    })
   6    export class AbcPipe implements PipeTransform {
```

Generated custom pipe code has a value parameter added by default. Use this core parameter to play with and implement logic around this parameter. With the generated default code, the return value is null.

```
transform(value: any, ...args: any[]): any {
  return null;
}
```

Add the logic to the return using the value parameter. In the example below, consider returning a (value * 100) for the pipe transform.

```
import { Pipe, PipeTransform } from '@angular/core';

@Pipe({
  name: 'abc'
})
export class AbcPipe implements PipeTransform {

  transform(value: any, ...args: any[]): any {
    return (value*100);
  }

}
```

After the implementation of successful pipe logic, it is now the time to use the pipe in the HTML file to view the result. Use the 'abc' pipe to any value on the HTML file.

```
<h1>
    {{625 | abc}}
</h1>
```

As the custom pipe logic applied to the value 625, the value multiplied by 100 results 62500. The browser displays the output as 62500.

62500

Integrating with the API

Targets for this Hour

- Integrating UI With The API
- Syntax to Integrate API

HOW TO INTEGRATE UI WITH THE API

As an Angular web developer, one should interact with the API team to get the required URLs for consuming the data needed. Developers should understand the syntax and the process of using API URLs in Angular code. Use the below syntax to consume API in the web application. The following step is to use the API URL in the below syntax. Bind the API result to the UI. Please follow the previous chapter examples on how to work with objects and lists to bind data on the UI. The API consumed result from the syntax is an object or a list in many cases.

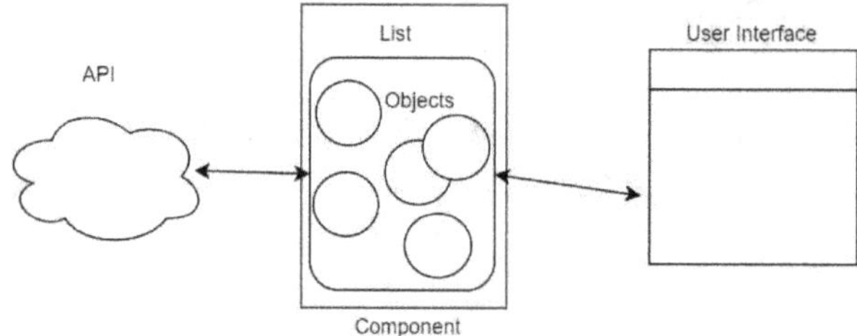

Consider a simple example below and sketch the steps to implement API integration.

1. Add HTML button code with a click event

2. Add the click event to the button 'Get'.

3. Add a function 'get_API_data()' to the component code.

4. Trigger this function when the user clicks on the button.

5. Import 'HttpClient' to work with API operations like get, put, post, delete.

6. Use 'httpClient.operation' like, get, or post to invoke the required operation.

7. Inside the function, use code 'httpClient.get(URL)' to get values from the API URL. To get data from the API, use 'httpClient.get'. To post data or to insert data to the API, use 'httpClient.post'. Similarly, to update, use 'put', and to delete, use 'delete'.

8. Create a variable MyApiResultData to store the output from the API. Use subscribe to get the complete data instead of partial data.

```
app.component.ts ✕      <> app.component.html

esthttp > src > app > TS app.component.ts > ↳ AppComponent > ⊘ get_AP
 1    import { Component } from '@angular/core';
 2    import { HttpClient } from '@angular/common/http';
 3
 4    @Component({
 5      selector: 'app-root',
 6      templateUrl: './app.component.html',
 7      styleUrls: ['./app.component.css']
 8    })
 9    export class AppComponent {
10
11      constructor(private httpClient: HttpClient) { }
12
13      private MyApiResultData = [];
14      private uri = 'API URL GIVEN BY API TEAM';
15
16      get_API_data() {
17        this.httpClient.get(this.uri)
18          .subscribe((pulledData: any[]) => {
19
20            this.MyApiResultData = pulledData;
21
22          });
23      }
24
25
26    }
```

9. To display data on the UI, the developer must study the structure of the object or list and use double curly braces to display the result.

```
TS app.component.ts          <> app.component.html  ×

testhttp > src > app > <> app.component.html > ...
  1    Testing
  2    <button (click)="get_API_data()">GET</button>
  3
  4    {{MyApiResultData[0].xxxxxxxxxxxxxxxx}}
  5    {{MyApiResultData[0].yyyyyyyyyyyyyyyyy}}
  6    |
```

Focus on live API integration is explained in the upcoming chapters.

Bitcoin Live Mini Project

Targets for this Hour

- Connecting to Live Bitcoin API
- Display Bitcoin Value on the UI

The target for this phase is to work on a live API integration code to pull the latest bitcoin price.

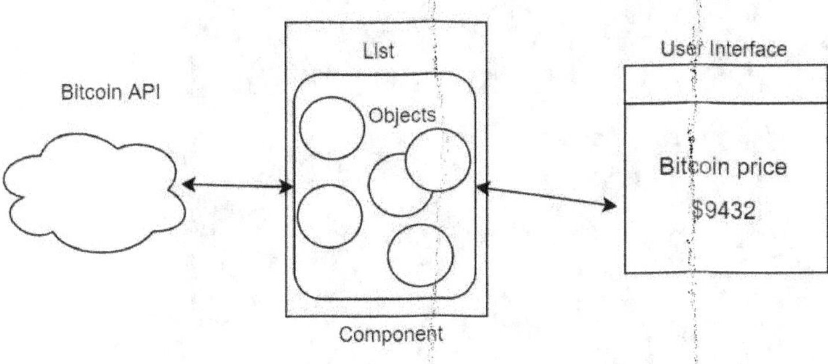

CALLING API IN THE COMPONENT

The first step is to get the API URL from the API team. In this case, consider using a live API URL. Based on the syntax to get API results from the previous chapter, follow the below steps to call API in the component. Refer to the below screenshot with code.

1. Create a variable 'uri' to store the live API URL.

2. Create a function 'get_API_data' to add code to talk to API, subscribe, and store the API result.
3. Import HttpClient from @Angular/common/http
4. Declare httpClient in constructor
5. Declare 'MyApiResultData' to store API result data.
6. Implement the logic to connect to API using httpClient.get(apiUrl)
7. Use subscribe to store complete results to 'MyApiResultData.'

```
TS app.component.ts  ✕      <> app.component.html

testhttp > src > app > TS app.component.ts > ᵗ AppComponent > ⚙ uri
  1    import { Component } from '@angular/core';
  2    import { HttpClient } from '@angular/common/http';
  3
  4    @Component({
  5      selector: 'app-root',
  6      templateUrl: './app.component.html',
  7      styleUrls: ['./app.component.css']
  8    })
  9    export class AppComponent {
 10
 11      constructor(private httpClient: HttpClient) { }
 12
 13      private MyApiResultData = [];
 14      private uri = 'https://api.coindesk.com/v1/bpi/currentprice.json';
 15
 16      get_API_data() {
 17        this.httpClient.get(this.uri)
 18          .subscribe((pulledData: any[]) => {
 19
 20            this.MyApiResultData = pulledData;
 21
 22          });
 23      }
 24
 25
 26    }
```

DISPLAYING API RESULTS IN THE CONSOLE

Based on the above steps, the result of API can be displayed in the console to verify the success of the data pull. Angular developers can play with console logs to manage the result object or list. Add the console.log at a required place in the code as below.

```
17      this.httpClient.get(this.uri)
18        .subscribe((pulledData: any[]) => {
19          console.log(pulledData);
20          this.MyApiResultData = pulledData;
21
```

```
TS app.component.ts  X      <> app.component.html

testhttp > src > app > TS app.component.ts > AppComponent > get_API_data > subscribe() callback
 1    import { Component } from '@angular/core';
 2    import { HttpClient } from '@angular/common/http';
 3
 4    @Component({
 5      selector: 'app-root',
 6      templateUrl: './app.component.html',
 7      styleUrls: ['./app.component.css']
 8    })
 9    export class AppComponent {
10
11      constructor(private httpClient: HttpClient) { }
12
13      private MyApiResultData = [];
14      private uri = 'https://api.coindesk.com/v1/bpi/currentprice.json';
15
16      get_API_data() {
17        this.httpClient.get(this.uri)
18          .subscribe((pulledData: any[]) => {
19            console.log(pulledData);
20            this.MyApiResultData = pulledData;
21
22          });
23      }
24
25    }
```

In the below screenshot, the console displays a complete API result. To view console in the browser like chrome, use 'F12' key or right-click on the browser and select 'Inspect'. Based on the result in the console, the developer can identify the parent-child object info to display on the UI.

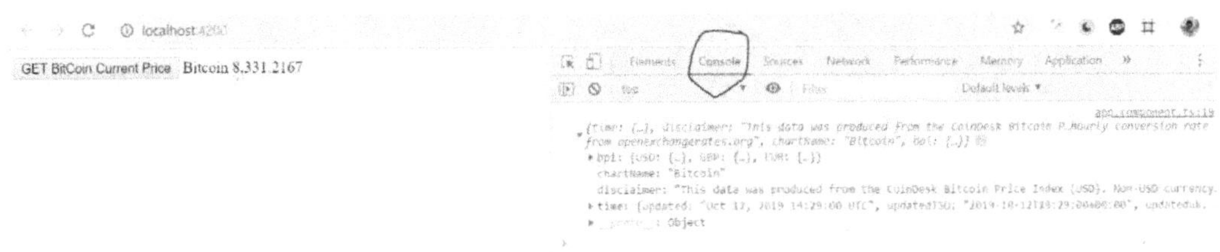

Expand the objects to view the child items. Expand till the developer locates the value to display on the UI. Capture the hierarchy to use in the HTML code.

Consider a situation where the requirement is to show the bitcoin rate on the webpage, then based on the below-expanded result, the hierarchy is 'bpi.USD.rate'. The hierarchy figured out should be appended to the API result object and use to display in the HTML code inside double curly braces.

DISPLAYING API RESULTS ON THE UI

As mentioned above, please follow the chapter 'working with objects and lists' to deal with data binding on UI. The result of the API call is an object or list in many cases. Follow the steps below to display results on UI.

```
TS app.component.ts          <> app.component.html ×

testhttp > src > app > <> app.component.html > ...
1
2    <button (click)="get_API_data()">GET BitCoin Current Price</button>
3
4    {{MyApiResultData.chartName}}
5    {{MyApiResultData.bpi.USD.rate}}
```

Run the application in the terminal. Once the user clicks on the 'Get BitCoin Current Price' button in the browser, the live bitcoin rate is displayed.

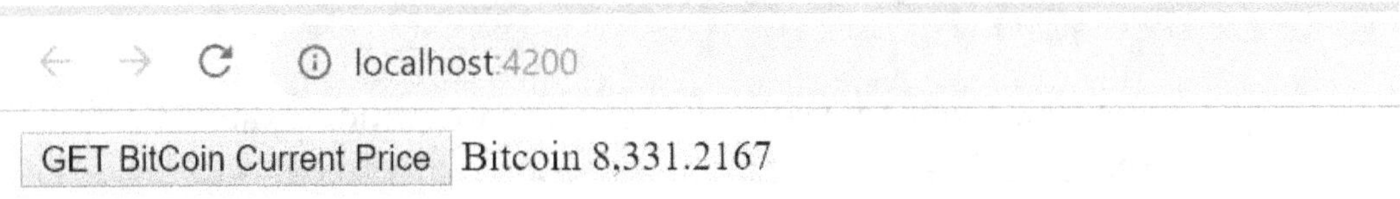

GitHub Live Users Mini Project

Targets for this Hour

- Connecting to Live GitHub API
- Display GitHub Users Details on the UI

The target for this phase is to work on a live API integration example to pull a few real GitHub users. The idea behind this second mini project is to make sure to practice and expertise similar live API integration development.

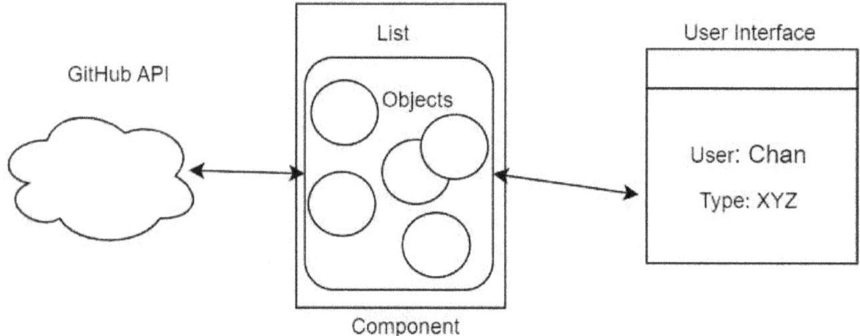

CALLING API IN THE COMPONENT

Get the API URL from the API team. In this case, connect to live GitHub API. Based on the syntax, follow the steps as the previous chapter to call API in the component.

1. Create a variable 'uri' to store the live API URL.

2. Create a function 'get_API_data' to add code to talk to API, subscribe, and store the API result.
3. Import HttpClient from @Angular/common/http
4. Declare httpClient in constructor
5. Declare 'MyApiResultData' to store API result data.
6. Implement the logic to connect to API using httpClient.get(apiUrl)
7. Use subscribe to store complete results to 'MyApiResultData.'

```typescript
TS app.component.ts X    <> app.component.html

testhttp > src > app > TS app.component.ts > AppComponent > uri
 1    import { Component } from '@angular/core';
 2    import { HttpClient } from '@angular/common/http';
 3
 4    @Component({
 5      selector: 'app-root',
 6      templateUrl: './app.component.html',
 7      styleUrls: ['./app.component.css']
 8    })
 9    export class AppComponent {
10
11      constructor(private httpClient: HttpClient) { }
12
13      private MyApiResultData = [];
14      private uri = 'https://api.github.com/users?page=6&per_page=2';
15
16      get_API_data() {
17        this.httpClient.get(this.uri)
18          .subscribe((pulledData: any[]) => {
19            console.log(pulledData);
20            this.MyApiResultData = pulledData;
21
22          });
23      }
24
25    }
```

DISPLAYING API RESULTS IN THE CONSOLE

Based on the above steps, the result of API can be displayed in the console to verify the success of the data pull. Angular developers can play with console logs to manage the result object or list.

```typescript
17        this.httpClient.get(this.uri)
18          .subscribe((pulledData: any[]) => {
19            console.log(pulledData);
20            this.MyApiResultData = pulledData;
21
```

Add the console.log at a required place in the code as below.

```
TS app.component.ts ✕    <> app.component.html

testhttp > src > app > TS app.component.ts > ᵗ AppComponent > ⊗ get_API_data > ⊗ sub
 1    import { Component } from '@angular/core';
 2    import { HttpClient } from '@angular/common/http';
 3
 4    @Component({
 5      selector: 'app-root',
 6      templateUrl: './app.component.html',
 7      styleUrls: ['./app.component.css']
 8    })
 9    export class AppComponent {
10
11      constructor(private httpClient: HttpClient) { }
12
13      private MyApiResultData = [];
14      private uri = 'https://api.github.com/users?page=6&per_page=2';
15
16      get_API_data() {
17        this.httpClient.get(this.uri)
18          .subscribe((pulledData: any[]) => {
19          console.log(pulledData);
20            this.MyApiResultData = pulledData;
21
22        });
23      }
24
25    }
```

Expand the console object or list and find the hierarchy to display username and type.

```
Elements   Console   Sources   Network   Performance   Memory   Application   »        ⋮  ✕

top                    ▼  ⊙  Filter                    Default levels ▼                      ⚙

                                                                        app.component.ts:19
▼ (2) [{…}, {…}]
  ▼ 0:
      avatar_url: "https://avatars0.githubusercontent.com/u/1?v=4"
      events_url: "https://api.github.com/users/mojombo/events{/privacy}"
      followers_url: "https://api.github.com/users/mojombo/followers"
      following_url: "https://api.github.com/users/mojombo/following{/other_user}"
      gists_url: "https://api.github.com/users/mojombo/gists{/gist_id}"
      gravatar_id: ""
      html_url: "https://github.com/mojombo"
      id: 1
      login: "mojombo"
      node_id: "MDQ6VXNlcjE="
      organizations_url: "https://api.github.com/users/mojombo/orgs"
      received_events_url: "https://api.github.com/users/mojombo/received_events"
      repos_url: "https://api.github.com/users/mojombo/repos"
      site_admin: false
      starred_url: "https://api.github.com/users/mojombo/starred{/owner}{/repo}"
      subscriptions_url: "https://api.github.com/users/mojombo/subscriptions"
      type: "User"
      url: "https://api.github.com/users/mojombo"
    ▶ __proto__: Object
  ▶ 1: {login: "defunkt", id: 2, node_id: "MDQ6VXNlcjI=", avatar_url: "https://avatars0.githubusercon…
    length: 2
  ▶ __proto__: Array(0)
```

DISPLAYING API RESULTS ON THE UI

Based on the figured-out hierarchy, the next step is to binding data on the UI. The result of the API call is an object or list in many cases. Use the hierarchy inside double curly braces in related HTML code to display results on the UI. After application execution in the terminal, the web page displays real GitHub user name and user type.

```
TS app.component.ts        <> app.component.html ✕

testhttp > src > app > <> app.component.html > ⬡ button
  1
  2    <button (click)="get_API_data()">GET Github User</button>
  3
  4    {{MyApiResultData[0].login}}
  5    {{MyApiResultData[0].type}}
```

Customer Care Mini Project

Targets for this Hour

- Understanding Customer Care Project
- Developing Customer Care Application
- Assignment

SCHEMATICS

With all the above experience, the target for this phase is to create a simple customer care application. Every project starts with requirements. Considering that, the first step is to frame some simple requirements for this project.

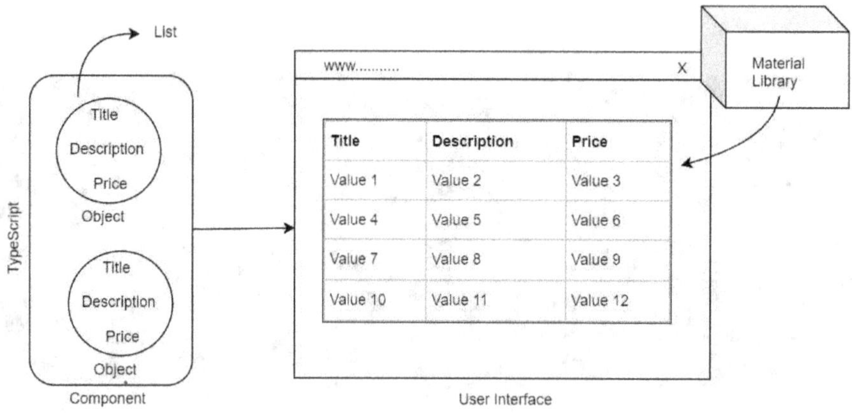

Customer care web application should have a web page with all complaints on the home page. The page should have a search option so that that customer care executive can filter complaints. To summarize, this mini-project should serve as a web application for customer care executives to view and filter complaints when a user calls them.

Based on the below mini-project sketch, the next step is to plan development for this requirement. Below are the work items to implement.

- Good looking table to display complaints
- Sorting for table
- Paging for table
- Search textbox and a button
- Filter table logic

Buchiki Customer Care

type user name

Check User Complaints

Id	Name	Complaint
1	Parthav	Incoming calls not working
2	Abhinav	Balance deducted with out using
3	Thanveer	New sim activation failed
4	Aadya	Unable to unlock phone
5	Aavyan	Unable to recharge

Items per page: 50 ▼   1 – 5 of 5   ‹

COMMANDS AND DEVELOPING THE APPLICATION

The first step is to use the material to create a good-looking table. To add material to the application, run a few commands. Run the below command in the terminal.

Command: ng add @angular/material

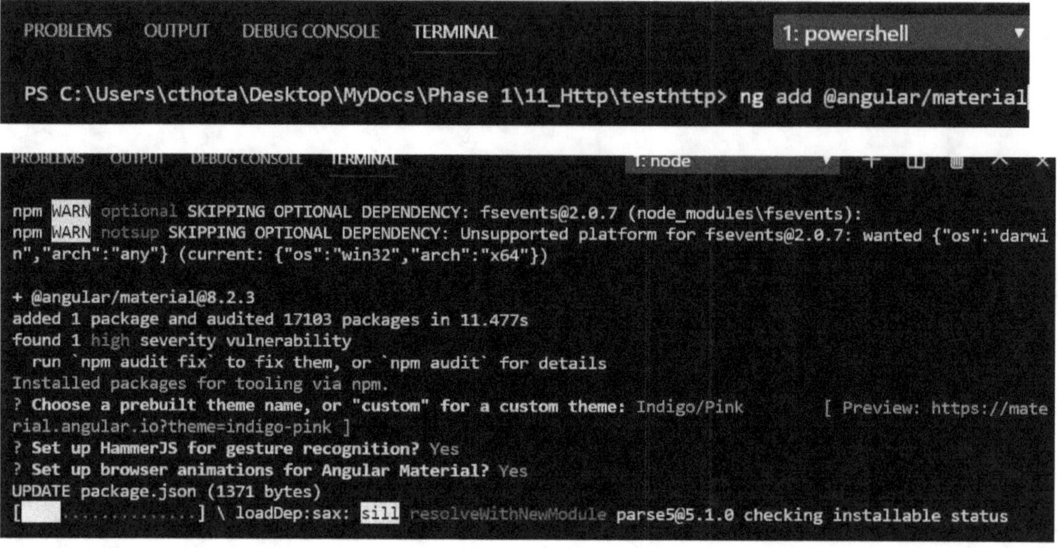

After adding material, the next step is to add the table using the below command.

Syntax: ng generate @Angular/material:table MyComponentname
Command: ng generate @Angular/material:table CustomerCareComplaints

This command generates a table component with the name given in the command. Use the selector on the web page at the targeted location in HTML to display the table. In this example, 'app-customer-care-complaints' is the selector in the related component file.

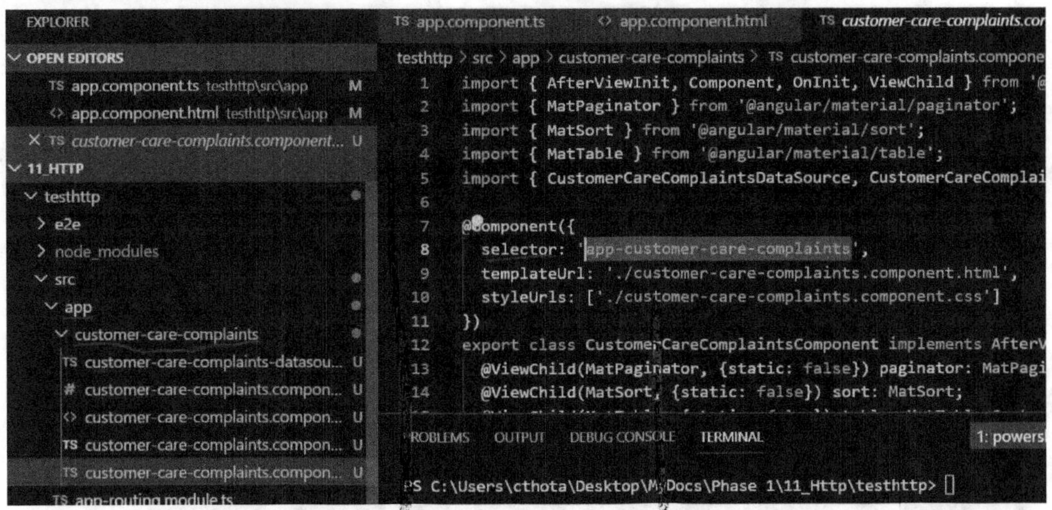

Use the selector as below in the app.component.html file. The below code displays the table on the browser as output.

```html
<app-customer-care-complaints>

</app-customer-care-complaints>
```

Run the application using 'ng serve –open'. The web page displays the result. Interestingly webpage shows some dummy data which is hardcoded in related 'datasource.ts' file. Check all required areas to update the code.

```
PROBLEMS   OUTPUT   DEBUG CONSOLE   TERMINAL                    1: node           ▼  +  ⊡  🗑  ∧  ×

PS C:\Users\cthota\Desktop\MyDocs\Phase 1\11_Http\testhttp> ng serve --open
 10% building 3/3 modules 0 active i [wds]: Project is running at http://localhost:4200/webpack-dev-server/
i [wds]: webpack output is served from /
i [wds]: 404s will fallback to //index.html

chunk {main} main.js, main.js.map (main) 23.5 kB [initial] [rendered]
chunk {polyfills} polyfills.js, polyfills.js.map (polyfills) 251 kB [initial] [rendered]
chunk {runtime} runtime.js, runtime.js.map (runtime) 6.09 kB [entry] [rendered]
chunk {styles} styles.js, styles.js.map (styles) 184 kB [initial] [rendered]
chunk {vendor} vendor.js, vendor.js.map (vendor) 5.7 MB [initial] [rendered]
Date: 2019-10-12T20:01:30.913Z - Hash: 0334766d3a858d40331a - Time: 8895ms
** Angular Live Development Server is listening on localhost:4200, open your browser on http://localhost:4
200/ **
i [wdm]: Compiled successfully.
```

```typescript
TS app.component.ts ×    <> app.component.html       TS customer-care-complaints.component.ts ×

testhttp > src > app > customer-care-complaints > TS customer-care-complaints.component.ts > CustomerCareCompla

12   export class CustomerCareComplaintsComponent implements AfterViewInit, OnInit {
13     @ViewChild(MatPaginator, {static: false}) paginator: MatPaginator;
14     @ViewChild(MatSort, {static: false}) sort: MatSort;
15     @ViewChild(MatTable, {static: false}) table: MatTable<CustomerCareComplaintsItem>;
16     dataSource: CustomerCareComplaintsDataSource;
17
18     /** Columns displayed in the table. Columns IDs can be added, removed, or reordered
19     displayedColumns = ['id', 'name'];
20
21     ngOnInit() {
22       this.dataSource = new CustomerCareComplaintsDataSource();
23     }
24
25     ngAfterViewInit() {
26       this.dataSource.sort = this.sort;
27       this.dataSource.paginator = this.paginator;
28       this.table.dataSource = this.dataSource;
29     }
30   }
```

Update data in the data source file with the required information as below. The data added here can be static or from the API call. Based on the previous API integration chapters experience, play with data in the data source file to make this static data to dynamic data.

```
TS app.component.ts        <> app.component.html        TS customer-care-complaints-datasource.ts  ×

testhttp > src > app > customer-care-complaints > TS customer-care-complaints-datasource.ts > [∅] EXAMPLE_DA
 7     // TODO: Replace this with your own data model type
 8     export interface CustomerCareComplaintsItem {
 9       name: string;
10       id: number;
11     }
12
13     // TODO: replace this with real data from your application
14     const EXAMPLE_DATA: CustomerCareComplaintsItem[] = [
15       {id: 1, name: 'Hydrogen'},
16       {id: 2, name: 'Helium'},
17       {id: 3, name: 'Lithium'},
18       {id: 4, name: 'Beryllium'},
19       {id: 5, name: 'Boron'}
20
21     ];
22
23     /**
```

The output on the browser looks like the below.

Id	Name
1	Hydrogen
2	Helium
3	Lithium
4	Beryllium
5	Boron

Items per page: 50   1 – 5 of 5

Change data to the required list instead of the data provided by the generated component. Update the related data source file with the required data. Add the complaints list with Id, User, Complaint.

```
      // TODO: Replace this with your own data model type
  8   export interface CustomerCareComplaintsItem {
  9     user: string;
 10     id: number;
 11     complaint: string;
 12   }
 13
 14   // TODO: replace this with real data from your application
 15   const EXAMPLE_DATA: CustomerCareComplaintsItem[] = [
 16     {id: 1, user: 'Parthav', complaint:'Incoming calls not working'},
 17     {id: 2, user: 'Abhinav', complaint:'Balance deducted with out using'},
 18     {id: 3, user: 'Thanveer', complaint:'New sim activation failed'},
 19     {id: 4, user: 'Aadya', complaint:'Unable to unlock phone'},
 20     {id: 5, user: 'Aavyan', complaint:'Unable to recharge'}
 21
 22   ];
```

Update the code related to displaying the table rows and columns in the associated HTML file. In this example, the file to update is 'customer-care-complaints.component.html'.

```
  1   <div class="mat-elevation-z8">
  2     <table mat-table class="full-width-table" matSort aria-label="Elements">
  3       <!-- Id Column -->
  4       <ng-container matColumnDef="id">
  5         <th mat-header-cell *matHeaderCellDef mat-sort-header>Id</th>
  6         <td mat-cell *matCellDef="let row">{{row.id}}</td>
  7       </ng-container>
  8
  9       <!-- complaint Column -->
 10       <ng-container matColumnDef="complaint">
 11         <th mat-header-cell *matHeaderCellDef mat-sort-header>Complaint</th>
 12         <td mat-cell *matCellDef="let row">{{row.complaint}}</td>
 13       </ng-container>
 14
 15       <!-- Name Column -->
 16       <ng-container matColumnDef="name">
 17         <th mat-header-cell *matHeaderCellDef mat-sort-header>Name</th>
 18         <td mat-cell *matCellDef="let row">{{row.user}}</td>
 19       </ng-container>
 20
```

Update the required code in the component file to read all new columns.

```
8        selector: 'app-customer-care-complaints',
9        templateUrl: './customer-care-complaints.component.html',
10       styleUrls: ['./customer-care-complaints.component.css']
11   })
12   export class CustomerCareComplaintsComponent implements AfterViewInit
13       @ViewChild(MatPaginator, {static: false}) paginator: MatPaginator;
14       @ViewChild(MatSort, {static: false}) sort: MatSort;
15       @ViewChild(MatTable, {static: false}) table: MatTable<CustomerCareC
16       dataSource: CustomerCareComplaintsDataSource;
17
18       /** Columns displayed in the table. Columns IDs can be added, remov
19       displayedColumns = ['id', 'name', 'complaint'];
20
21       ngOnInit() {
22           this.dataSource = new CustomerCareComplaintsDataSource();
23       }
```

Run the application with 'ng serve –open' command. The output in the browser looks like the below.

Id	Name	Complaint
1	Parthav	Incoming calls not working
2	Abhinav	Balance deducted with out using
3	Thanveer	New sim activation failed
4	Aadya	Unable to unlock phone
5	Aavyan	Unable to recharge

Items per page: 50   1 – 5 of 5

After the successful implementation of the complaints table, the next step is to add the header, search box filter to the application. Add a simple header with an h2 tag, a name for the application.

```
<h2>
   Buchiki Customer Care
</h2>
```

And the output in the browser appears like the below.

Buchiki Customer Care

Id	Name	Complaint
1	Parthav	Incoming calls not working
2	Abhinav	Balance deducted with out using
3	Thanveer	New sim activation failed
4	Aadya	Unable to unlock phone
5	Aavyan	Unable to recharge

Items per page: 50   1 – 5 of 5   <   >

The next step is to add a textbox and a button in the HTML code. Use input and button HTML tags to create a search box and a button. Run the application in the terminal using command 'ng serve –open' to view output in the browser.

```html
<h2>
  Buchiki Customer Care
</h2>

<p>
  <input type="text" placeholder="type user name" >
</p>

<p>
  <button>Check User Complaints</button>
</p>
```

The output looks like the below

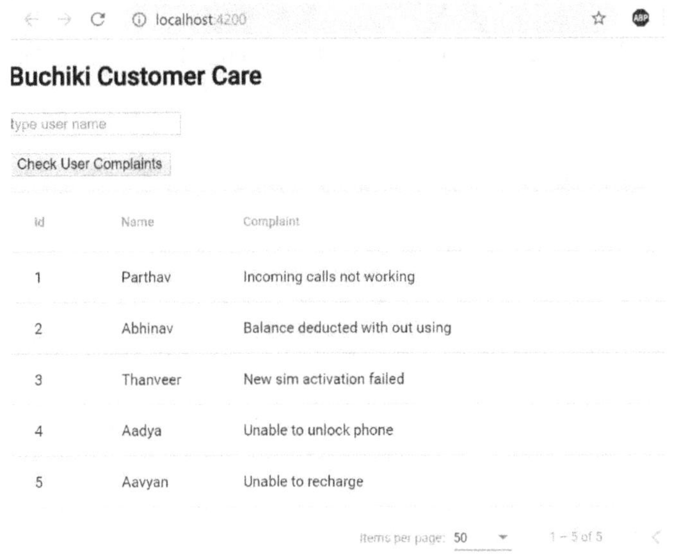

Buchiki Customer Care

Id	Name	Complaint
1	Parthav	Incoming calls not working
2	Abhinav	Balance deducted with out using
3	Thanveer	New sim activation failed
4	Aadya	Unable to unlock phone
5	Aavyan	Unable to recharge

Use a filter with an arrow function, which considers include scenario with a static value.

Syntax: CompleteData.filter
(anything => anything.columns.filtertype('something'))

```
ponent.html ×    Ts customer-care-complaints.component.ts        Ts customer-care-complaints-datasource.ts ×
http > src > app > customer-care-complaints > Ts customer-care-complaints-datasource.ts > Ts CustomerCareComplaints
11      complaint: string;
12    }
13
14    // TODO: replace this with real data from your application
15    const EXAMPLE_DATA: CustomerCareComplaintsItem[] = [
16      {id: 1, user: 'Parthav', complaint:'Incoming calls not working'},
17      {id: 2, user: 'Abhinav', complaint:'Balance deducted with out using'},
18      {id: 3, user: 'Thanveer', complaint:'New sim activation failed'},
19      {id: 4, user: 'Aadya', complaint:'Unable to unlock phone'},
20      {id: 5, user: 'Aavyan', complaint:'Unable to recharge'}
21
22    ];
23
24    /**
25     * Data source for the CustomerCareComplaints view. This class should
26     * encapsulate all logic for fetching and manipulating the displayed data
27     * (including sorting, pagination, and filtering).
28     */
29    export class CustomerCareComplaintsDataSource extends DataSource<CustomerCareComplaintsI
30      data: CustomerCareComplaintsItem[] = EXAMPLE_DATA.filter(p=>p.user.includes('A'));
```

Output in the browser shows only records based on the specified filter. In this example, it shows complaints with the **user has 'a' in their name.**

Buchiki Customer Care

Id	Name	Complaint
2	Abhinav	Balance deducted with out using
4	Aadya	Unable to unlock phone
5	Aavyan	Unable to recharge

ASSIGNMENT

Its time to test the skills based on the learning experience. Here is a small assignment to crack. Figure out the solution on how to pass value from UI to the component filter. The task is to replace the **static value 'a'** to a value retrieved from the search textbox.

Debugging Code

Targets for this Hour

- How to Debug Code

HOW TO DEBUG

Developing an Angular web application is one part, and fixing issues in the existing application is the other part of the developer's responsibility. The developer's responsibility in debugging code is to figure out the code flow and play with variables and its values while the application execution is in progress, fix the issue.

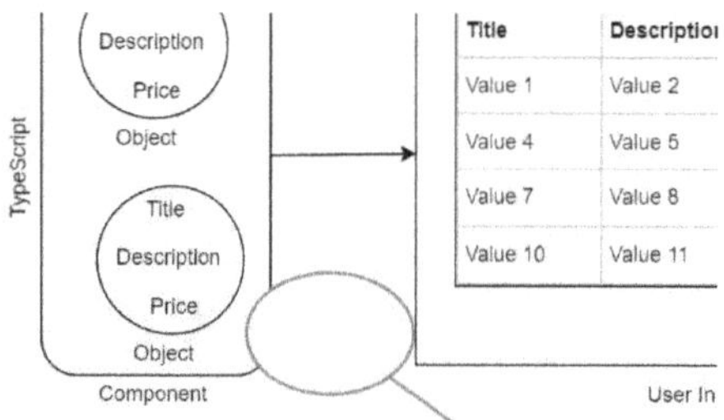

The developer must identify all the areas in code, mainly where debugging is required. Add the word 'debugger' at the required area in the code. Run the application in the web browser. When the output is on the web browser, right-click on the browser, select inspect to open developer tools. Refresh the browser and do the required operation in the browser. If the code has events, then trigger the event to hit the breakpoint at the debugger.

```
TS app.component.ts ×

src > app > TS app.component.ts > ฿ AppComponent > 🔧 num1
  5        templateUrl: './app.component.html',
  6        styleUrls: ['./app.component.css']
  7     })
  8     export class AppComponent {
  9
 10        num1: number = 0;        You, a few seconds ago
 11        num2: number = 0;
 12        res: number = 0;
 13
 14        Mul() {
 15           debugger;
 16           alert('test');
 17           this.res = this.num1 * this.num2;
 18        }
 19     }
```

In developer tools, code stops at a point where the developer sets the breakpoint using the debugger. Rollover mouse on the variables at that point to see values during the application execution. Checking variable values at the run time helps developers debug the issue and add fixes where required.

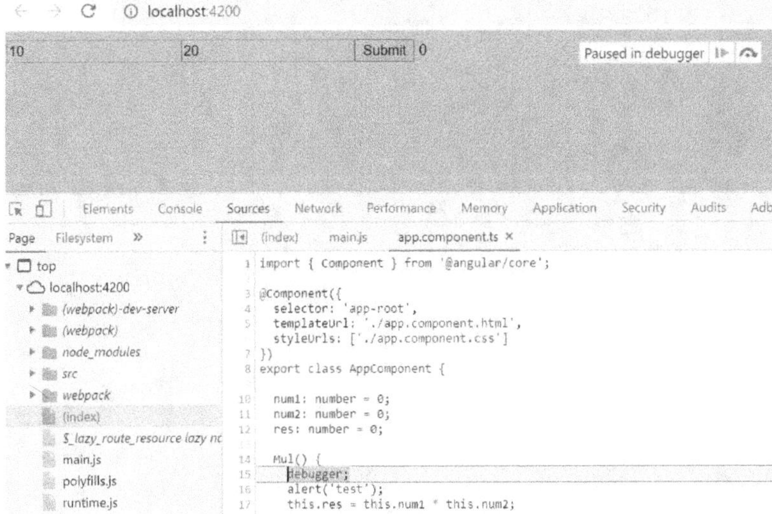

Add values to watch during the debugging process to debug and play with the results.

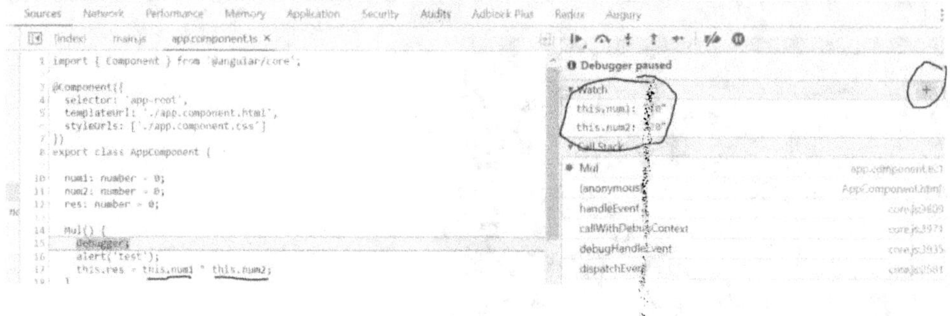

Next Steps

Targets for this Hour

- Steps for Advanced Angular Development

NEXT STEPS TO ANALYZE

In addition to the learnings from 24 hours, the suggestion is to analyze and explore the below topics online. Below advanced topics will add extra grip on the advanced Angular development concepts. Angular experts recommend working on one example each from the below research items.

Advanced routing techniques

How to add router links
How to add redirect route
How to add a parameterized route

Get, Insert, Delete, Update operations with API.

How to post data to API from UI
How to Update data in UI talking to API
How to delete data from UI talking to API

Implementing error handling

How to use console logs
How to use 'catchError'
How to use try/catch
How to use handleError

RXJS, state management for Angular applications

Go through docs, get started sections in rxjs website

Automated deployment using Jenkins, Azure

Create and deploy one Angular web application using Jenkins
Create and deploy one Angular web application using Jenkins

End to End application development, including database operations

Create an online web application like customer care with UI, API, Database

Logging mechanisms

Check npm for different logging packages available for Angular
Refer to ngx-logger module

Working with modules

Create an Angular web application with more than one module.
Analyze module configurations.

Angular Libraries

Create an angular library and make it available to the public via npm.